D1829166

THE SMALL PLACE

The Purple and Yellow Border when the Tulips, Doronicums, Camassias, and Ground Covers are all in Bloom.

THE SMALL PLACE

ITS LANDSCAPE ARCHITECTURE

Elsa Rehmann

WESTHOLME
Yardley

Originally published by G. P. Putnam Sons in 1918

Westholme Publishing, LLC
Eight Harvey Avenue
Yardley, Pennsylvania 19067
Visit our Web site at www.westholmepublishing.com

First Printing: April 2008
10 9 8 7 6 5 4 3 2 1

ISBN: 978-1-59416-066-0
ISBN 10: 1-59416-066-X

Printed in United States of America on 50 percent post-consumer recycled paper.

IN MEMORY OF MY FATHER

CARL F. REHMANN

AN ARCHITECT

PREFACE

The idea for this book grew out of an intensive study of the small place from the point of view of the landscape architect. The actual formation of the book began several years ago while I was still serving my "apprenticeship" and much of the material was gathered on the occasional journeys for observation to town and country with which I varied the work in the office. During this time I have studied and worked on large gardens and rich estates and I take unusual pleasure in the opportunities for landscape development that they offer; but the small place still retains its fascination, for its possibilities, which are generally overlooked, are infinite, and its limitations, which are considered as drawbacks, ought to be the very means of its making.

INTRODUCTION

I HAVE selected fifteen problems in landscape architecture to show in a simple and popular manner the fundamentals that underlie the planning and planting of the small place. I have made my selection from the work of landscape architects,—the majority of them belong to the American Society of Landscape Architects,—so that each problem would have a logical plan and a firm structural foundation with the planting developed as a decorative component.

I have taken great care in the selection of these problems. I tried to use only places that have a complete and well organized plan. It is difficult to find places—especially small ones—in which all the parts are given a proportionate share in the development and where these parts are grouped to form a harmonious whole, for the attainment of perfection in a plan or underlying structure is often not understood or entirely overlooked by the layman, who is only attracted by the beauty of an individual plant or by the gayety of a flower. A perfect plan grows, moreover, out of existing conditions, out of the limitations and peculiarities of the site and soil, and out of the requirements of the owner and of his domestic and social needs. In the few cases where I have used only a part of a complete layout, the part under discussion seemed complete enough in itself to warrant it.

I have used only problems which have arrived at such a degree of completion or growth that the designer's ideas can be easily grasped by the layman. I have used only those problems in which the designer's ideas have been actually carried out. In search of these I have made many a useless journey, for many of the places that I visited had been either entirely neglected or never completed or changed out of recognition. The design is seldom altogether lost but the planting is often subject to changes, for the client seldom realizes that in a carefully considered plan each plant has its special value in the development of the entire scheme.

No matter how much thought and ingenuity the landscape architect expends in evolving a layout, it is a matter of time and growth before the pictures in the designer's mind materialize. It is, therefore, very essential that the owner is willing to coöperate sympathetically with the designer, to obtain a comprehensive understanding of what the design means and of what the ultimate results are to be. It is to such coöperation that Mr. DeForest, for instance, lays the success of his design.

It is of equal importance—especially in the case of flower planting—that the client understands the worth of the designer's supervision, not only while the work is being done but also during its growth. A share in the success of Miss Coffin's problem is due to the owner's appreciation of the need of her occasional visits of inspection—several are made each year—when all the little planting details are looked after so that the garden retains its perennial charm without a single lapse.

These fifteen problems are of such diversity in design and planting that they exhibit many principles of landscape art as they are applied to the small place. They emphasize the fact that while all problems are governed by the same laws, each demands an individual treatment. I considered it valuable, therefore, to give a chapter to each problem. Each chapter is illustrated with a plan and with enough pictures to vivify the essential points of each problem. The description of the planting is given in detail for the discussion of concrete examples seems of greater value than mere generalities. I hope that the reader, as he studies each problem in its entirety, will, perchance, conceive his own property as one complete and consistent design and shape its individuality according to the laws of landscape art.

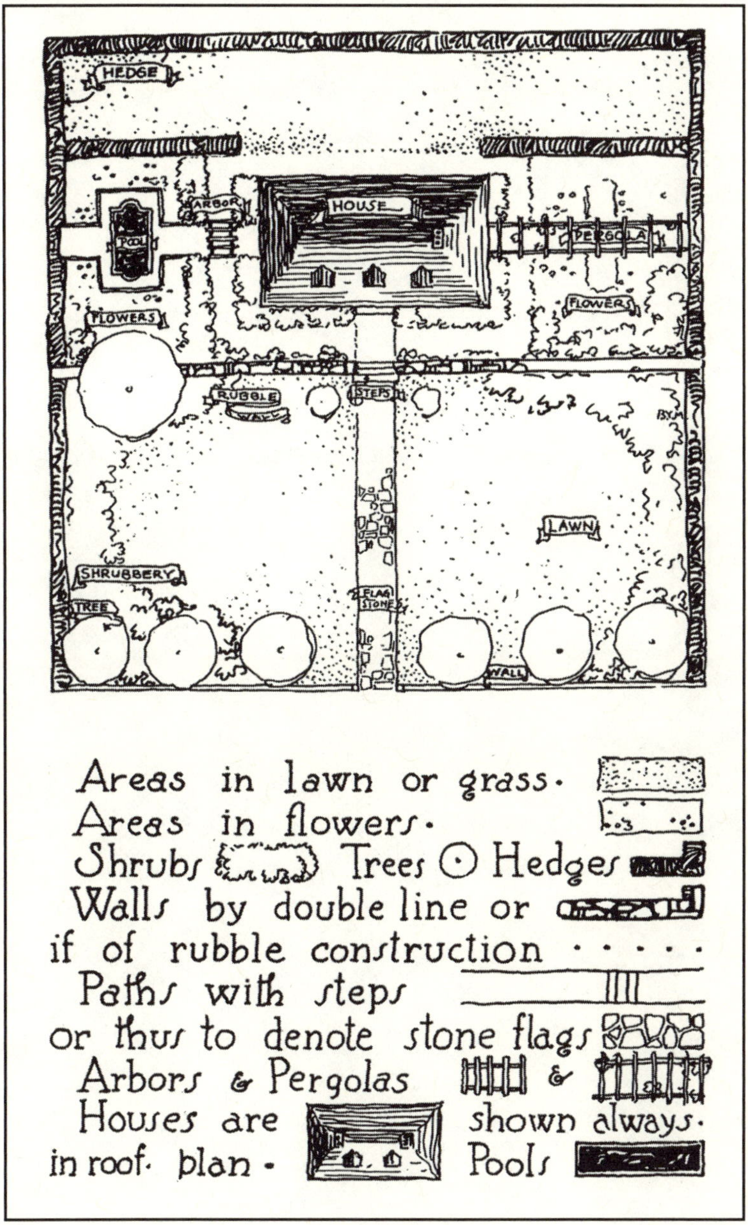

The Key to the Plans.

The arrows on the plans indicate the point of view of the photographs.

CONTENTS

PROBLEM I

PROBLEM II

PROBLEM III

PROBLEM IV

PROBLEM V

CONTENTS

CONTENTS

PROBLEM XIII

PROBLEM XIV

PROBLEM XV

ILLUSTRATIONS

ILLUSTRATIONS

ILLUSTRATIONS

ILLUSTRATIONS

ILLUSTRATIONS

ILLUSTRATIONS

THE SMALL PLACE

PROBLEM I

A COMPREHENSIVE LAYOUT FOR A CITY PROPERTY, BY SIBLEY C. SMITH, LANDSCAPE ARCHITECT, PROVIDENCE, R. I.

This property is located at Providence, R. I. Its dimensions are 140 x 209 feet

THE development of this city lot illustrates the comprehensive use that can be made of a small piece of ground. The house stands in the very center of the property. There is a drive on the north side which passes right by the entrance porch. On the east a shrubbery-bordered lawn makes a pleasant outlook for the living room. On the south the conservatory leads to the terrace and to the flower garden. On the west in back of the house is the laundry yard and next to it the stable court, which connects with the drive again. The various parts are united and framed in by a wall built around the entire property. In this way privacy and seclusion are obtained in the very midst of the city.

THE SMALL PLACE

The house is only open from September until June. It is during this time that the grounds can be enjoyed by the family. And it is for this reason that the planting is so chosen and arranged that it will produce its best effects during the late fall, winter, and early spring. There are late autumn flowers and shrubs with brilliant foliage. There are evergreens and shrubs with berries and gayly colored stems. There are spring bulbs and early flowering shrubs. These give abundant green and bright color to the city garden during the cold seasons of the year.

The drive was made as practical as possible. It runs parallel to the house and turns abruptly with short curves to the two entrances. Its shape fits the ground and the rising grade of the street and the two gateways make easy the entrance and departure of vehicles. The door of the stable, placed on the axis of the straight part of the drive, makes an easy connection between stable, front door, and street.

It is here that the initial impression of the grounds and the house is received. The planting has been carefully considered in order to obtain at the very beginning a certain distinction char-

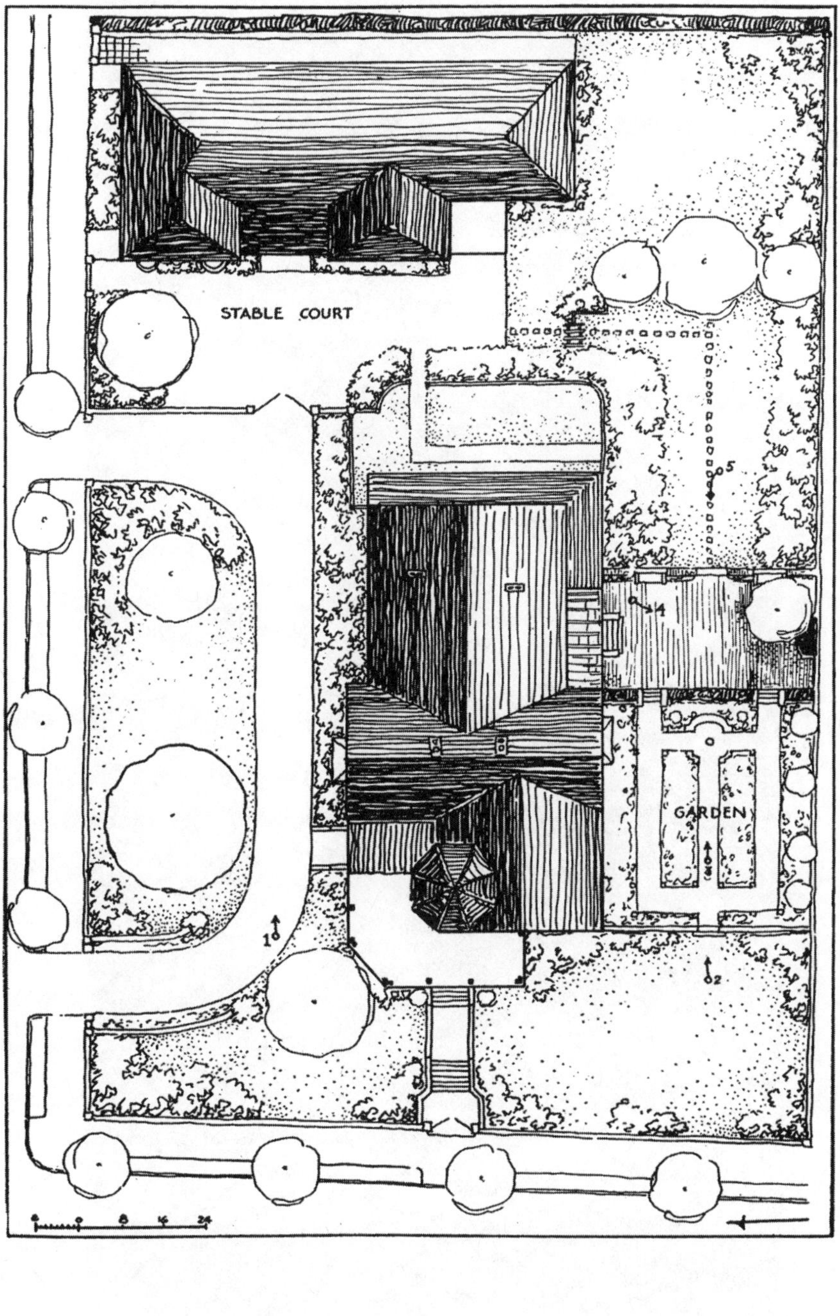

The Plan.

The Drive.

acteristic of the entire place. An old Beech with widespread branches dominates this part of the grounds. In its deep shade many woodsy, shade-loving plants like Ferns, Solomon's Seal, Uvularia, and Violets make a ground cover where grass will not grow. The drive is bordered by narrow planting strips. On one side Myrtle is planted near the entrance, then Ivy, and near the exit a group of Fragrant Bush-Honeysuckles. Along the wall in back of this strip there is Regel's Privet in scattered groups. On the other side of the drive near the entrance are *Euonymus radicans*, Fragrant Sumac, Pachysandra, and Ivy, with Hemlock, Forsythia, and Dogwood against the wall in back of them. Along the house the planting is principally of Rhododendrons. It is interesting that these Rhododendrons, that did poorly in their original position on the south side of the house before the garden was built, flourish on the north side. They dislike excessive sunlight, especially in winter, but enjoy the more even temperature of the shade. Now they thrive every winter without any protection except a mulch around the roots. They look particularly pleasant in contrast to all the neighbors' Rhododendron beds, which are tied up in their coverings of evergreen boughs at the first approach of cold weather. *Leucothoë catesbæi*, *Pachysandra terminalis*, Ferns, Ivy, and Yellowroot make a foreground planting for the Rhododendrons. Along the wall of the service court Fragrant Sumac and Asters are planted, and *Ampelopsis Engelmanni*, which has clinging suckers like the Boston Ivy and a free growing habit like the Virginia Creeper, climbs over wall and posts.

All the plants on the drive endure northern exposure and shady positions. It is a planting composed mainly of evergreens. To the exclusion of all stiff specimen conifers, broad-leaved evergreens have been used. The decorative effectiveness of evergreen planting depends as much on the nicety with which the different varieties are combined as on the selection of the material. It is a planting chosen principally for its fine foliage effects. The lasting green of Myrtle and Ivy, Hemlock, Euonymus, and Pachysandra, the almost evergreen foliage of the Fragrant Bush-Honeysuckles, and the glossy leafage of the Rhododendrons give a splendid winter effect. Against these are contrasted the Leucothoë when its foliage turns a deep red in the autumn and the fall color of the Yellowroot and Fragrant Sumac.

From the drive we can pass to the lawn. It is a little place, quite private and secluded, six feet above the sidewalk. The wall around it has done away with the original steep grass slope which was never good to look at and very difficult to keep in order. By the building of this retaining wall, several feet were added to the width of the lawn, a desirable economy of floor space for a small piece of ground.

The shrubbery planted along the front wall is not put in a continuous border. With economy of space in mind and with a desire to show the wall between, the familiar *Spiræa Van Houttei*, Regel's Privet, and Hemlock are planted in groups at intervals. The Privet and Hemlock have a sweeping habit of branching, very desirable in plants for lawn enclosures. They provide a winter contrast of black berries against evergreen boughs. Japanese Quince is planted near the house for early spring bloom, and *Rosa multiflora*, climbing over the wall, has bright hips for autumn effect.

From the lawn we can enter the flower garden. It is quite a marvelous little place. In considering all that has been done in it, it is really worth while noticing that its size is only thirty-five by forty-five feet. Its slightly raised position above the front lawn and its sunken position in relation to the terrace gives it the change of level to which so many gardens owe a great deal of their charm. Part of its charm comes, too, from its enclosure, from the walls which frame the two sides of the terrace. Then, it gets the benefit of the large Pine on the terrace and of the old Spruce in the back lawn.

The flower effects have been confined entirely to the spring and autumn months. In the spring the central beds glisten with the more delicately colored varieties of Darwin Tulips underplanted with Forget-me-nots. The side borders are filled with creamy white Narcissus and *Fritillaria meleagris* with a ground cover of pale lavender *Phlox stellaria.* Delicate pinkish white Japanese Anemones, replacing the Tulips in the central beds, begin the fall flowering. A mass of pale lavender Asters with white and yellow Snapdragons in the foreground fill the wall border, while yellow and maroon Chrysanthemums along the house continue the flowering season until after the frost.

In the planting of a small garden striking seasonal effects can be obtained only through large masses of a very limited variety of plants. This does not

The Garden Seen from the Lawn.

THE GARDEN IN TULIP TIME.

exclude, however, the use of many different kinds of plants in small clumps. Many are used in this garden, among them *Iris reticulata*, *Abelia rupestris*, *Lilium rubellum*, *Anemone blanda*, *Iris cristata*, *Crocus speciosus*, *Iberis sempervirens*, and *Helleborus nigra*. It is necessary, of course, to plant these many kinds in very small quantities, but this will not limit their effectiveness as they are seen at the closest range. They have to be subordinated, however, to the general seasonal effect and be in harmony with its color. The seasonal display here of Narcissus and Darwin Tulips in the spring, of Japanese Anemones, Asters, Snapdragons, and Chrysanthemums in the fall gives a unity not to be overlooked but strongly emphasized in the small garden.

In the design of the garden every effort was made to make it attractive during the cold months of the year. The space saved through the elimination of all summer blooming flowers has been used for a liberal planting of small evergreens. *Euonymus radicans*, kept closely clipped, forms the edging of the central beds. Andromeda, Laurel, Pachysandra, and the dainty *Daphne cneorum* make a narrow shrubbery along the wall. Japanese Yew, Japanese Holly, and Azalea are planted along the house wall. These shrubberies give a good color effect when in bloom, they make a background for the flowers, and they are especially valuable in giving a cheerful note to the garden in midwinter.

A broad brick-paved terrace adjoins the flower garden with everything to make it attractive during the cold weather. It is warm and sunny and dry under foot. Its walls catch and hold the heat of the sun and make it comfortable to sit in even late in the fall, while the Pine tree furnishes just enough shade to make it a pleasant afternoon lounging place even in the warm days of late spring. The terrace is sheltered on the north by the house, from which it is approached through a small conservatory. The stucco pilasters and wooden beams of the conservatory make it a desirable winter substitute for a pergola. On the west the terrace overlooks the flower garden. The other two sides are enclosed by walls. Opposite the conservatory the wall is raised to give privacy from the carriage drive of the adjoining lot. The monotony of a solid wall is changed into a feature of much interest by an arrangement of three panels. The side ones are filled with Della Robbia Singing Boys, the center one with a brick wall

The Terrace.

The Arch between the Back Lawn and the Terrace.

fountain. The fountain provides an architectural feature which is pleasing in its placing opposite the conservatory door and in its location near the Pine which overshadows it. A wall fountain is an economy of space and the smallest trickle of water has an enlivening effect in a garden. The three flat arch openings in the other wall allow the green of the back shrubbery to enter into the composition. This wall is unusual, in giving both the effect of seclusion and a suggestion of something of interest beyond. *Jasminum nudiflorum* planted under the conservatory windows has bright yellow flowers very early in the spring. Snowdrops, *Iris reticulata*, and English Primroses are planted in the sunny nooks at the foot of the wall and a white Chinese Wistaria climbs over it. The annual vine *Cobea scandens* gives a delightful lavender bloom in the fall and English Ivy planted on the shady sides provides the winter interest. The terrace is a pleasant out-of-door room. It is comparatively small but the wide-open view of the flower garden and the broken glimpses of the back lawn makes it quite big in feeling if not in actual extent.

The central arch of the wall is a door to the back lawn. On either side are informal shrubbery borders. The ground under the shrubs is planted with Bloodroots, Solomon's Seals, Trilliums, Crocuses, Squills, Violets and other spring flowers. It is a substitute for a rock or wild garden which shows what charming simple effects can be developed on a small place if thought is given to the intensive use of every corner. In the shrubbery itself the main masses are composed of Lilacs, Snowberries, *Euonymus alatus*, *Cornus alba*, and *Kerria japonica*. The Lilacs provide abundant spring bloom, the Snowberries a charming autumn touch. The brilliant red branches of the Cornus and the vivid green stems of the Kerria give a very effective winter contrast. At the farther end of the lawn the vista is terminated by a wonderful old Spruce backed by a semicircular lattice. A row of square white stepping stones leads from the terrace to the Spruce and turns at right angles to enter the stable court. Even in this court the winter effect has been thought of. There are Barberries with red berries and Privets with black fruit.

We have made a complete circuit of the grounds, just as I made it one sunny day in December. The visit was a timely one to show me how beautiful the garden was going to be during each winter month. It was fascinating to watch the gradual unfolding of each garden picture as I walked around the house. Every part of the property, every little corner, was utilized to its fullest extent, and beneath its decorative treatment the underlying plan bound together the various subdivisions into a closely interrelated and unified whole.

PROBLEM II

A Complete Layout—Within Small Dimensions, by Pray, Hubbard, and White, Landscape Architects, Boston, Mass.

Location—Allston, near Boston. Size—64 x 164 feet

THE development of this property was determined by the location of the path which now connects the front door with the street. Such a path is a necessity in daily use. It must be practical, dry under foot, and as direct as possible. These reasons, however, should not deprive it of interest. The very fact that it is in daily use is all the more reason why it should have beauty inwrought in the making.

The house had to be set high above the street level and had to accommodate its shape to the long narrow lot. The necessity of facing the house for these reasons upon an unpaved road, which is only a right of way, and the impracticability of placing the entrance to the grounds on it, forced this unconventional solution. The direct communication with the main thoroughfare, only a block away, through the use of the narrow street on the south of the house made it of practical importance to locate the entrance on this street. The problem still remained of how to get in an interesting but direct manner from the street to the front door.

The grounds are walled in along this street to avoid steep grass terraces. This wall is surmounted by a white picket fence and broken in the middle by the entrance steps. One step up from the street we stand on a small space in front of seven steps which are walled in on both sides by the retaining walls of lawn and flower garden. Once up these steps we come to a little vestibule or anteroom, if we may borrow the architect's terms. It is a little breathing space, a place pleasant to linger in a moment. It is the parting of the ways. Masses of Rhododendron with a background of Cedars face us. On the left the white gate opens into a short cut through the flower garden to the living room. On the right tall feathery *Retinispora pisifera* specimens on either side indicate that the walk continues in that direction toward the front door. After we pass these evergreen sentinels we make a turn and

Problem II.

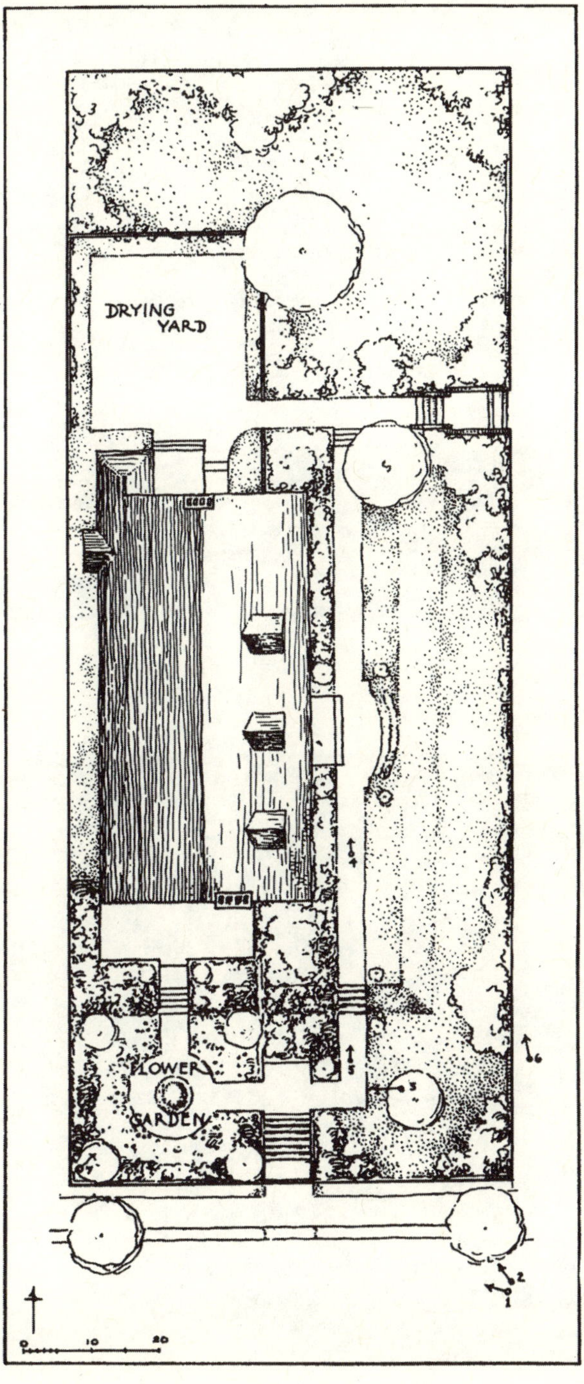

The Plan.

Problem II. No. 1.

The Grounds Seen from the Street.

Problem II. No. 2.

The Enclosure.

another five steps bring us up to the house level. This turn and the shrubbery around it hide one flight of steps from the other and the level piece of ground between breaks into two short flights what might have been one tiresome as well as tiring flight of steps. Once on the house level the walk runs along the whole front of the house. Not only is this arrangement of the walk direct and attractive in itself but it makes possible a considerable space of unbroken lawn between the walk and the fence along the unpaved road. This solution seems so simple and appropriate that all the care, labor, and study put into the planning for grading, for construction of wall work and steps is entirely lost to mind. It should be so. All study should be hidden behind seemingly unstudied naturalness. Such fundamental planning, to which the planting, so important in itself, is added as a decorative feature, displays the ingenuity of the landscape architect and shows the practicability of employing him.

The path is laid in brick. Brick pavements have a permanent decorative quality and a warm color which is of special value in the winter effectiveness of a garden. At the end of the path stands an old Maple. It is a piece of rare good fortune to have it just in that position. Such a tall old tree has a peculiar manner of imparting some of its own dignity and distinction to the house and the grounds near it. It has a depth of shadow which has an indescribable charm. It provides a strong contrast of shade to the sunny lawn.

The house is well orientated in relation to the various parts of the grounds. It faces east upon the lawn. On the south is the living porch facing the garden. On the north the kitchen and cellar doors open on a lattice-screened and brick-paved enclosure used both as laundry yard and service court. A path which joins at right angles the path along the front of the house connects this court with the roadway.

The corner of the lawn by this service path is planted with Rhododendrons, Lilacs, and Forsythia. The Rhododendrons find an appropriate place in the shade of the Maple. Next to them are the Lilacs, then the Forsythia. The heavy plain leaves of the Lilacs harmonize exceptionally well in color and texture with the Rhododendron foliage. Both the Forsythia and the Lilacs keep

Problem II. No. 3.

The Vestibule.

The Entrance Path.

green late into the fall. Together they give three monthly periods of bloom. The arching branches of the Forsythia bring this shrubbery into character with the Lady Gay Roses climbing along the eastern fence. In front of the Roses are Peonies. These two give two long periods of bloom. Peonies like isolation from other flowers for complete development and are as valuable as shrubs in foliage effectiveness. Next come Poplars, then come groups of Lilacs, *Deutzia lemoine*, and *Spiræa Van Houttei*. This unbroken but irregular border hides the house from the street except where glimpses of doorway or arched window are seen through the branches. It gives a delightful informality to the grounds which characterizes so many of the older and larger places in the near vicinity of Boston.

Andromeda floribunda was originally planted along the house under the windows. It is one of the most pleasing of the dwarf evergreen shrubs. The buds of its white flowers have a curious way of appearing all winter long as if they were just ready to burst into bloom which helps to enliven the garden during the winter months. These plants have disappeared and the unfortunate placing of Box bushes to take their place spoils the continuity of the border. These Box bushes illustrate a frequent mistake in shrub planting for they were planted there simply by the caprice of the planter, who considered his plant material only at its own and separate value instead of at its valuation as a part of a well ordered design. The Rhododendrons and Cedars at either end of the house show how effective evergreens can be against red brick walls. Two Rose of Sharon bushes with double pink flowers frame the entrance porch. Their upright habit accentuates its quiet formality. Just this upright stiffness which makes it so difficult to mold it into shrubbery borders invests the Rose of Sharon with a peculiar fitness when it is used to produce architectural balance.

The planting along the house and for the lawn enclosure has been given in such detail to show how full of interest a little place can be when careful attention is given to the proper arrangement of shrubs as a boundary around a small lawn. Evergreens give it much winter interest, deciduous planting emphasizes the spring bloom. Then, after the Roses are through blooming in July, the lawn is framed by quiet greenery and the color interest is absorbed by the flower garden.

PROBLEM II. No. 5.

THE LAWN.

PROBLEM II. No. 6.

THE FENCE.

The Garden.

PRAY, HUBBARD, AND WHITE

The garden is a delightful little place not thirty feet square. It shows the infinite possibilities of the small flower garden. We like its friendly colors, its little touches of formality, and its seclusion above the street.

Part of the success of this garden is due to its enclosure. On the north side by the porch are masses of Rhododendron. Lily-of-the-Valley plants are crowded together by the steps, and there is a Box bush on either side. On the east side is the picket fence. Opposite is a row of Arbor Vitæ now six or eight feet high, and on the south side the branches of the street trees make a heavy green screen.

Much of the success of the garden comes from the worth of its design. In a small garden the design wins approval through sheer simplicity. This design is based on a circular composition inscribed in a square. It is an old motive always new. The spreading *Pinus mugho* is not a very acceptable central figure for it is coarse in texture and will soon grow too large and dwarf the rest of the design. We are sorry it is in the photograph for the center was the place designed for a sundial or a slender columned bird bowl.

Most of the success of a garden must be attributed to the choice and arrangement of the flowers. The succession of bloom creates a pleasurable perennial interest. The arrangement of the flowers emphasizes the circular composition. On the edge of the circular path are eight *Sedum spectabile.* In back of them are planted the tall lilac blue *Iris pallida dalmatica* interspersed with Anthemis, the Golden Marguerite. The third tier is composed of Daffodils and pink and white Phlox. Along the street wall are rows of Hollyhocks. In front of the green of the Arbor Vitæ light blue Larkspurs raise their slender spires in early summer and Aconitum, the Monkshood, gives a similar effect in autumn. On either side of the gate a bush of low *Deutzia gracilis* blossoms early in the spring and later in July two plants of Yellow Day Lilies placed on either side of the path to the house make bright spots of color. To complete the formal effect a white-flowering Rose of Sharon is planted at each corner. From the time the Narcissus comes out in April until the Rose of Sharon fades there is always something blooming in the garden. The middle of August, when the picture was taken, is the gala time. It is the climax of the season. The Rose of Sharon, the Sedum, and the Phlox are all blooming together. It is, however, not necessary, as it is not possible, to have so much bloom all the time to make the small garden effective. A little bloom goes a long way. When I saw it in early July with the Hemerocallis just beginning to bloom and the Larkspurs in flower, the garden was quite charming with its delicate touch of blue and gold. Even when it gets too cold to sit out-of-doors, the garden has lost little of its attractiveness. The Rhododendron foliage, the fragrant Box bushes, the pyramidal Arbor Vitæ, and the red brick of the paths provide much winter interest.

The enclosure, the architectural details, the design, the flowers, each has an important part to play. It is not in their separate parts but in their interrelated action toward garden effectiveness that their complete worth lies in the art of garden making.

PROBLEM III

AN INFORMAL ARRANGEMENT OF A WOODED PROPERTY, BY
E. GORTON DAVIS, LANDSCAPE ARCHITECT,
CORNELL UNIVERSITY, ITHACA, N. Y.

This property is located at Ithaca, N. Y. The main property is 110 x 136 feet. The "outside" garden is 90 x 110 feet

OPEN expanses of ornamented lawns which expose the full view of the house to every passer-by are of a past day in garden art. Vine-covered walls and fences, hedges, shrubbery borders, and slopes clothed with trailers and recumbent shrubs form the boundaries that are helping to make the attractive streets of to-day. Bare and uninterrupted views of houses are now replaced by pleasing impressions caught over hedges and through shrubbery. These enclosing frames make one comprehend the meaning of the English wall and hedge bounded gardens and appreciate the desirability of the privacy thus attained. The street boundary is not to be chosen hastily, for it must be in keeping with the style and character of the house and give the correct intimation of the grounds it encloses. It must not, however, be too different from the rest of the places on the street.

For this house and for these grounds, it seemed best to plant a Cedar hedge all along the street boundary. The gates for drive and walk entrances break the hedge line but preserve the continuity of the boundary. The tall unclipped Cedars that mark the main entrance and add variety of skyline to this point unite with others near them to give a picturesque quality to the entrance and thus strengthen the impression of simplicity desired in the grounds. *Rhodotypus kerrioides* has been planted along the outside of the hedge. The White Kerria has a pleasant delicacy to its white flowers, and its persistent black fruit is sprinkled lightly over the bush. Its unfortunate tendency to have yellow foliage is avoided by keeping it on the north side of the hedge, out of the sun. Incidentally, it makes a pleasing contrast for the clipped hedge. The stiffness of most clipped hedges could be easily relieved by some such low free growing planting. Not even on the inside is the hedge left entirely exposed. Along

Problem III.

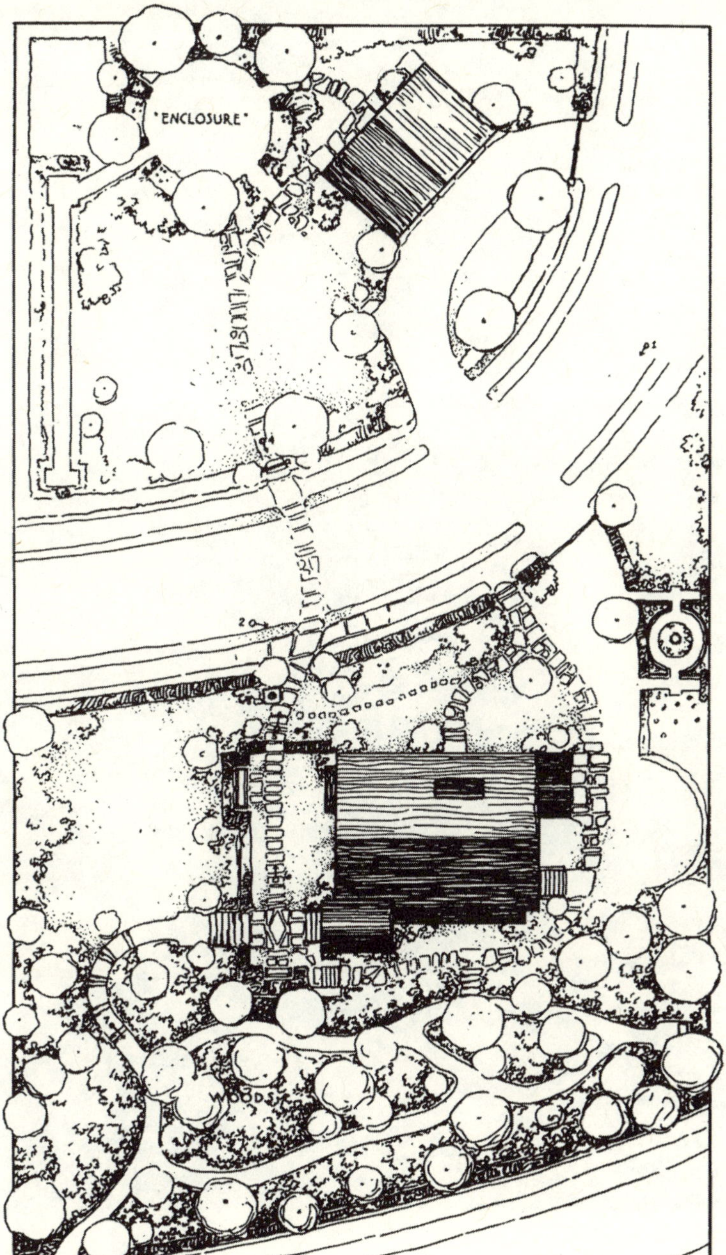

The Plan.

The Street View of the Grounds.

the lawn boundary Sweet Briar Roses are placed against the Cedars, and in front of the house the Cedars act as a background for an herbaceous border whose taller flowers overtop the hedge.

The passage between the street and the house is perhaps the most frequently used part of the grounds. It, therefore, ought to be a fitting approach to the front door, one that will be agreeable, day by day, to home-comers and one that will be a welcome to visitors. It ought to be an approach that will be in keeping with the style of the house, one that will express, too, in some way the manner of household living. It ought to be the very keynote that will give the correct initial impression of the entire place.

In this problem, it is necessary to pass along the entire side of the house to reach the entrance steps. At first,—before the work on the grounds was begun,—this walk was an ungainly procedure. From the street entrance you had to walk downgrade and then up again before you reached the porch. The ground was then graded in such a way that now you reach the porch across an eighteen-foot-wide terrace which affords a level and agreeable entrance. At first the house stood amid sloping ground and had an awkward and unstable look. Through this grading the house has gained a pleasing appearance of solidity. It is upon such underlying structural improvements—like this simple piece of grading—that many attractive features of small properties depend.

This level space has become more than an approach. It is a pleasant place for outdoor sitting. The slanting position of the gateway and the tall Cedars cut off all possibilities of a glimpse into the grounds. The hedge around the terrace is of globe-shaped Thuya,—it might have been of *Taxus cuspidata*,—which is low enough for pleasant views across the sloping lawn and into the woods on the back hillside. English Daisies, planted all along the hedge, give a homey little touch. The nice placing of the regular stepping stones of the path with the broad grass spaces on either side give the terrace a pleasing breadth. The wooden gateway and wooden seats, as well as the stepping stones, are appropriately used with this quiet house of gray stucco and shingle.

From the terrace broad field stone steps lead down to the lawn and then by easy grades to

Problem III. No. 2.

The Gate to the Terrace.

Problem III. No. 3.

In Front of the House. Inside the Cedar Hedge.

Problem III. No. 4.

The Gate of the Outside Garden.

Problem III. No. 5.

Inside the Gate of the Terrace with a Glimpse of the House Across the Road.

the wood paths. In the crevices of the stones many rock plants are tucked. There are Golden Tufts (*Alyssum saxatile compactum* and *A. rostratum*), dwarf silver toned *Anthemis aizoon*, Arabis, Thrift, dwarf Baby's Breath, delicate tinted Saxifragas, and all kinds of gay Sedums. This method of softening the stone and brightening the path with bits of flower color is an exquisite acquisition from English gardens.

The woods is roughly 50 by 150 feet in its entire area and yet its paths are of enough length to create a whole series of charming wood pictures along their sloping ways. Pines and Hemlocks, undergrowth shrubs and trees supplement the existing woods of Oaks, Hickories, and Maples. Dogwoods and Judas trees make a charming spring combination full of delicacy and color. Then there are Azaleas, the soft rose *Azalea nudiflora* and its brighter flame-toned relative, *Azalea calendulaceæ*. For early summer there are masses of Laurels scattered through the woods and at special places there are Rhododendrons, the tall native *Rhododendron maximum*, the smaller-leaved *Rhododendron carolinianum*, and the low small-flowered *Rhododendron myrtlefolium*. There are masses of Leucothoë and an occasional Yew

(*Taxus canadensis*). For the fall there are white-berried *Cornus paniculata*, *Viburnum acerfolium* with autumn-tinted maple-leaved foliage and black fruit, and Witch-hazels whose very late flowers and yellowed foliage herald the winter.

It would seem as if the picture were complete and yet these trees and shrubs form but a background for hundreds upon hundreds of plants that love wood soil and shade. All the early wild flowers are there, Bloodroots and Dutchman's Breeches, Hepatica and Spring Beauties, Arbutus and Partridge Berries, Columbines and wild Bleeding Hearts, Mandrakes and Wild Ginger. There are Violets and Trilliums in great variety, many kinds of Lady Slippers (Cypripediums, Habanarias, *Orchis spectabilis*) and a complete collection of ferns. There are Solomon's Seals and Mertensias, groups of *Cimicifuga racemosa* (the white Snakeroot), and bold masses of Eupatoriums and wild Asters. There are Bluets and wild blue Lupines and lilac blue *Phlox divaricata*. Monarda (the Bee Balm) makes a bright spot of color, orange and red Wood Lilies (*Lilium candense*, *Lilium philadelphicum*, and *Lilium superbum*) are growing in gay masses, and in more secluded and sheltered

The Terrace.

Problem III. No. 7.

The Woods.

nooks an occasional Cardinal Flower gleams scarlet amid the deep green of the woods.

The gathering and collecting of these wood plants has become a pleasant hobby, all the more worthy because the placing and composing of the plants in their woodsy setting has been done with such care that it is in harmony with the structural integrity of the whole place.

The segment-shaped piece of land on the other side of the street was bought to prevent the possibility of any objectionable building rising in front of the house. A charming chalet, too picturesque, perhaps, to be in keeping with the modest old-fashioned air of the residence, was built upon it. Part of it is used by the owner as an office. The placing of this house, in a subordinate position on the side of the grounds, allows ample room for landscape development. In front is a roomy lawn, on one side is a long walk with a flower border that acts as a cutting garden, and tucked away into the back corner is a small salad garden. The main feature is the circular flower enclosure. It is connected by a direct walk with the house terrace across the road and so becomes an integral part of the main grounds.

This additional garden space is really what the Germans call an "Abseits Garten" or a garden outside. It originated in old towns where the houses were so huddled together within the walls that the gardens had to be planted, necessarily, outside the fortifications. Here, the "outside garden" is so close to the house that the careful placing of entrances and gateways brings the two properties together into one logical and structural whole.

PROBLEM IV

A Colonial Fore-court and Garden of a Farmhouse, by Arthur A. Shurtleff, Landscape Architect, Boston, Mass.

This property is located at Shrewsbury, near Worcester, Mass. The dimensions of the Fore-court are 42 x 65 feet; those of the Garden are 34 x 38 feet

The Fore-court.

THE house stands in the midst of fields in a small community in Massachusetts, not far from Boston. The walled-in fore-court or dooryard was designed to separate the house grounds from the wide farm lands on every side. It is an approach or introductory passage from the road to the house door. The drive and roads to the barns are thus separated from the main entrance to the house.

It is a well kept level place. The stone walls make a strong dividing line between its smooth lawns and the rougher ground without and are in keeping with the farm surroundings. The picket fence in front, with the small posts, is in keeping with the colonial character of the house. Ampelopsis is growing over the wall to soften its surface. Lilacs are massed at the corners near the road, Mock Oranges are grouped near the entrance gate, and Poplars are placed in two balancing groups just outside the wall near the corners of the house. At the entrance gate stands a great Ash with an enormous spread of branches. It dwarfs the house and creates the homey impression so often unconsciously attained in old farmyards through the planting of one large tree near the front door. Here, it stands so far from the house that it does not demand the sacrifice of light usual in the older examples. The old Apple trees, inside the yard, are pleasant features that add to its simplicity. The narrow flower borders along the inside of the wall are composed of a very few kinds of plants such as early Yellow Day Lilies, Madonna Lilies, Larkspurs, and Phlox. They are planted not with the idea of producing a carefully arranged border that would attract particular attention but with the idea of breaking up the long straight wall surface with a few interesting plants whose color would be refreshing against the gray of the stone. As the fore-court

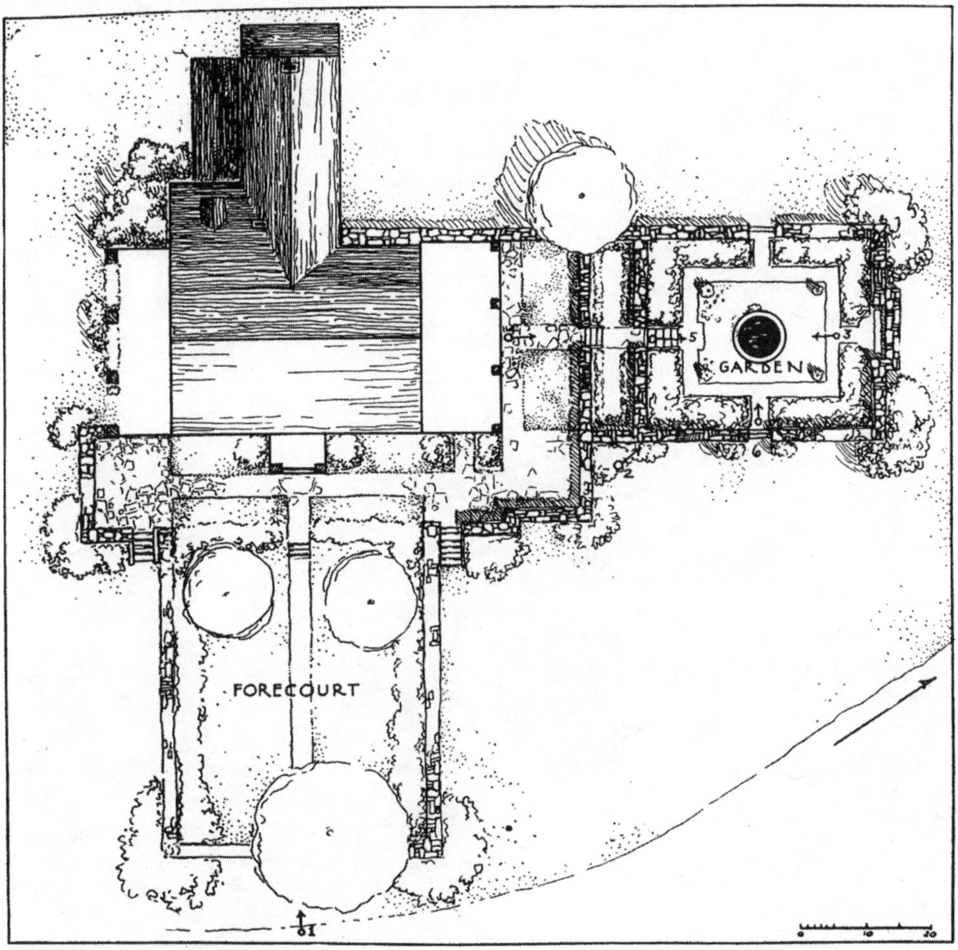

The Plan.

The Fore-Court.

is considered merely as an approach, a place to walk through and not a garden to linger in, it is essential to make it simple enough in arrangement so that it can be grasped in its entirety at the first glance.

This fore-court, placed here to conform with the colonial style of the house, is an interesting free interpretation of an old colonial garden form. The front doorway garden, as it was found in old New England and is still sparingly seen in conservative communities, is a form derived from the English fore-court, of which the English doorway garden is a humbler, more intimate, and less formal expression. In these colonial examples, the front fence stood near the road and the side fences extended back to the corners of the house. It was, therefore, rectangular in shape, taking its dimensions from the width of the house and the distance it was placed back from the road. At first, the enclosure of the colonial fore-yard had a purely practical reason for existence. It preserved from the inroads of cattle a little clearing where the housewife could grow a few flowers. But soon it became something more. There was an attempt to create a little air of formality for the approach to the front door. There was a nice striving to separate the small orderly garden from the rougher fields and the bigger expanses of surrounding country. These same reasons inspired its repetition for this country house. In its simple arrangement, there is a message to every dweller in rural communities, a suggestion of how to give the farmhouse a worthy dignity through an appropriate setting.

THE GARDEN.

To one side of the house, the ground slopes quite steeply and a small garden was won from the surrounding farm lands by giving it three levels. Highest is the terrace outside the living room porch. Going down five steep stone steps we stop on a narrow strip, not more than ten feet wide, where Roses grow and tumble over the wall. Down another five steps and we stand in the garden proper.

It is a very small garden. It is walled in with the same field stone used in the enclosure of the fore-court. An adequate enclosure is one of the main essentials of a garden. By shutting it in, the garden is relieved of the disturbing task of competing with the bigness of the surrounding country with its varied nature. The trees that

The Garden.

The Three Levels of the Garden.

arch over the wall add much to the interest of the enclosure. The charming hooded seat built into the wall reminds one of seats in sheltered corners of English gardens. Without the two arched gateways the garden might have seemed a little cramped. The round pool in the center of the garden is little larger than a bird bowl but it is in perfect scale. The Japanese Iris are grouped around the pool and the specimen Mugho Pines make accents for the corners of the grass plot. The flower borders are very narrow, and the flowers are necessarily few, but they are of sufficient variety to be incidents in the summer. When I saw them early in July, two great Peony bushes marked either side of the seat, the white Japanese Iris was in full bloom, the Foxgloves had just faded, the Larkspurs were beginning to open, and a very little early pink Phlox had just come out.

This garden has all the requisite elements, proper enclosure, flower borders, grass plot, pool and seat, and ought to be suggestive to the owners of farmhouses where gardens can only be had if they need the minimum of upkeep and attention. It ought to be suggestive as well to the owners of small city properties who generally despair of having gardens because they lack spacious grounds, unlimited means, and gardening inclinations. It hints at the possibilities of the small garden for which there is ample need and opportunity in our towns and suburbs.

The Garden Seen from the House.

Problem IV. No. 5.

The Sheltered Seat.

Problem IV. No. 6.

One of the Gateways.

PROBLEM V

THE PLANTING OF AN APPROACH AND DRIVE TURN, BY OLMSTED BROTHERS, LANDSCAPE ARCHITECTS, BROOKLINE, MASS.

This property is located at Chestnut Hill, Pa.

WHILE this house is a large country home with very interesting terraces and gardens, its approach and drive turn can be appropriately considered in the planting of a small place. The house is suggestive of the large English houses with its long irregular plan, its series of mullioned windows, and its many-gabled roof.

All along its front, following the curving line of the drive, there is a hedging of clipped Box and a few tall unclipped Box bushes are grouped in a windowless corner. Such uniformity in the planting along the house walls manifests reserve but it is necessary to accompany it by planting which will relieve its regularity. So, Honeysuckle, Ivy, and Euonymus are creeping up the stucco walls, a pink climbing Hybrid Tea Rose has reached the second story window above the rough stone which forms the stair well, and Pachysandra, the lovely evergreen ground cover, interplanted with Christmas Roses, makes a charming edging in front of the Box.

The oval inside the drive turn is dominated by the Beech. Ivy, Euonymus, Myrtle, and the dwarf St. John's Wort, *Hypericum calycinum*, creep in a great spreading mat around the broad trunk of the tree. On one side Andromedas are planted, the low *Andromeda floribunda* and its more graceful relative *Andromeda japonica*. On the other side of the intertwining vines are dwarf *Rhododendron Wilsoni* which have lovely small pink flowers and next to them are *Azalea indica alba* which are crowned with heavy clusters of white flowers. Just beyond, around the turn to the left, two young White Pines spread their horizontal branches over Yews and Andromedas, *Pinus mugho*, and a few Barberries. In among this planting, groups of Junipers raise their slender columns: *Juniperus virginiana*, the Common Red Cedar, *Juniperus Kosteri*, and *Juniperus chinensis*, with nice variation in their green, gray, and silver foliage tones. Beyond, yet farther around the

Problem V.

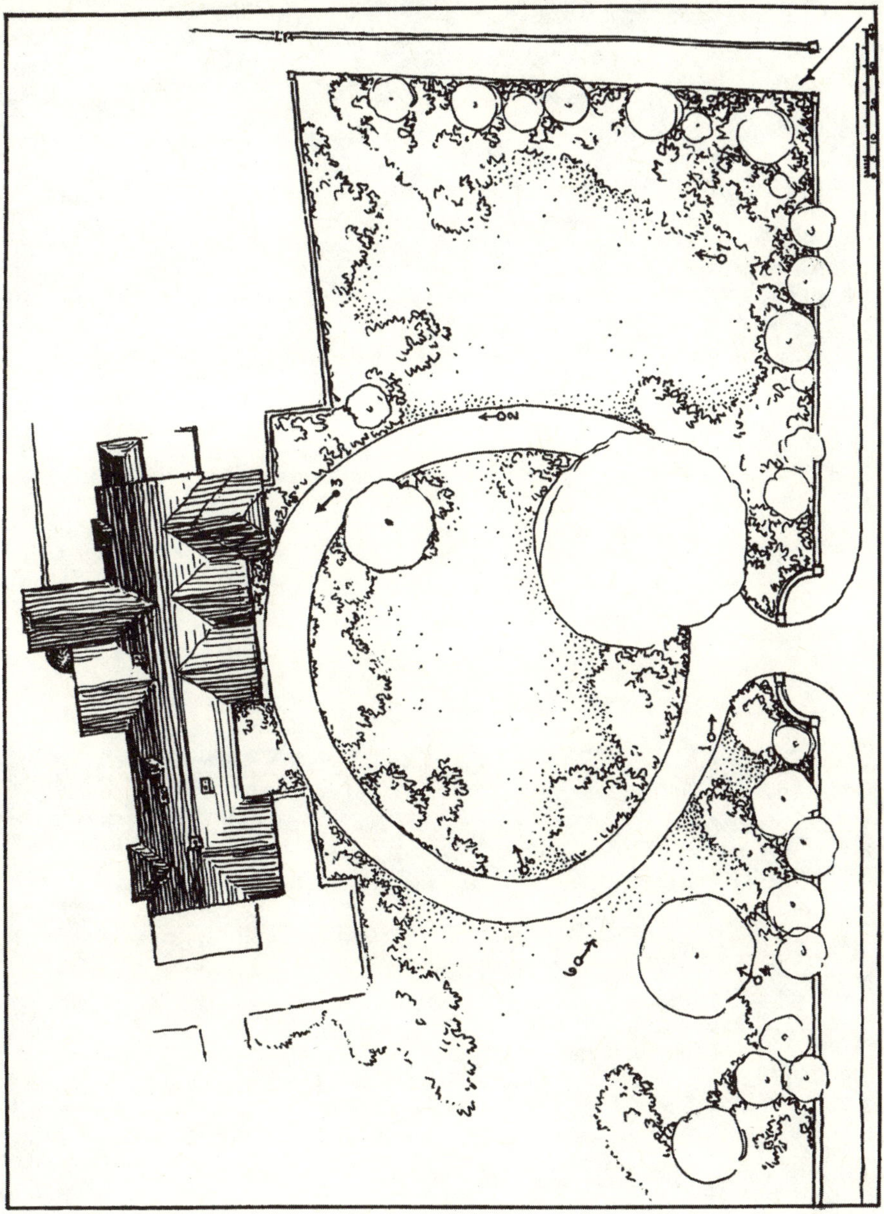

The Plan.

Problem V. No. 1.

The Great Beech.

Problem V. No. 2.

The Drive nearing the House.

turn opposite the entrance porch, groups of slender *Juniperus Schotti* spring up out of a low planting of Andromedas, *Azalea hinodegiri* with its delicate foliage and flat branching, and *Spiræa thunbergii*. In the next segment, amid Azaleas, Yews, and Mahonias, the pyramidal Junipers appear again, scattered, as before, in longish irregular groups, but the interest of this planting is centered upon a group of four Dwarf Horse-Chestnuts, *Æsculus parviflora*, with their effective palmate leaves and tall plume-like flower spikes. This planting has a varied and intimate character in contrast to the planting of the bays and of the outer edges of the drive which is marked by a big simplicity.

To the left of the gateway, native Rhododendrons form the background for Laurels, Andromedas, Mahonias, and *Azalea arborescens*, with a few *Azalea calendulacæa* for a bright color touch. Where this border turns to become the enclosure of the larger lawn a big group of Tree Lilacs makes an excellent accent in the shrubbery. Their tall white flowers are very striking and their large and heavy oval leaves harmonize with the broad-leaved evergreens.

Rhododendrons form the dominant planting of

the other bay and act as a unifying factor. Masses of native Rose Bay are placed in back of hybrid varieties. There are crimson Rhododendron "Parsons," pink Rhododendron "H. Sargent," and white *Rhododendron album elegans*. They are arranged in a continuous easy flowing line around the bay. Where the boundary rounds in toward the gateway the Rhododendron masses merge into Laurels and these give place to dwarf *Rhododendron Wilsoni*. Where the planting approaches the house, the Rhododendrons are supplanted by *Azalea hinodegiri* and by the lovely *Azalea indica alba*. A few *Magnolia stellata* and Cedars are placed in back of them, the lovely Magnolia flowers acting as forerunners to the even lovelier bloom of white Azaleas.

This planting offers flower effects of great beauty. Take, for example, the Andromedas with tender white sprays, the pure white Azaleas, the delicate Laurels, the brilliant Rhododendrons. Each effect is distributed through the various sections of the planting. Besides, emphatic color spots are provided, here by a group of bright *Azalea hinodegiri*, there by a few starry Magnolias, here by a cluster of Dwarf Horse-Chestnuts, there by a mass of Tree

Problem V. No. 3.

At the Entrance Porch.

Problem V. No. 4.

The House.

Problem V. No. 5.

Inside the Oval.

Problem V. No. 6.

Near the Gate.

Lilacs. But the flower effects, attractive as they are, act only as color incidents amid the prevailing green of the evergreen planting.

The planting offers an interesting diversity of forms. The graceful drooping habit of *Andromeda japonica*, the flat branching of the Yews, the torchlike shoots of the *Pinus mugho*, the compact growth of the Box, the conical shapes of the Cedars, give variation to the strong billowy form of the Rhododendron masses.

The big entire oval leaves of the Rhododendron are arranged in large paintable clusters. In harmony with them, through a similarity of foliage, shape, and structure, are Laurels, white Azaleas, Andromedas, Myrtle, Euonymus, Magnolias, and Tree Lilacs. These give the dominant foliage note. Amid them Mahonia with spiny dentated leaves, Spiræa with feathery foliage, White Pines with soft needle clusters, Pachysandra and Christmas Roses and Dwarf Horse-Chestnuts make pleasing deviations.

The planting is composed almost entirely of evergreens. The green of their persistent foliage becomes the prevailing color of the approach, which is in consequence cool, restful, and quiet, but in such a complexity of planting, green appears in all its manifold shades. Take, for meager example, the somber Rhododendron green and contrast it with the varying greens of the different Junipers or with the light delicate green of *Spiræa thunbergii*. With each additional variety, the color complexity increases, but, by delicate adjustment, the tone of one green mass merges into and mingles with that of the adjoining one. The blending of the light and dark tones, together with the delicate mottling of sunlight and shadow, gives the approach a wonderful charm.

Wonderful as the planting is, it does not exist for itself alone. House, approach, and planting are considered as component parts of one big scheme. This triple coördination is one of great subtlety and each problem demands individual treatment. Therefore, the charm of this planting lies in the fact that it interprets and emphasizes the atmosphere of the house and the essential character of the approach.[1]

[1] I wish to mention that I obtained the use of this problem through the kindness of Mr. James Frederick Dawson, an Associate Member of the firm of Olmsted Brothers, who was particularly interested in the development of this place.

The Rhododendrons.

PROBLEM VI.

PROBLEM VI

A SIMPLE HOME-GROUND, BY PRAY, HUBBARD, AND WHITE, LANDSCAPE ARCHITECTS, BOSTON, MASS.

This property is located at Fall River, Mass. Its dimensions are 100 x 250 feet.

WITH an inborn knowledge of garden art and land economy, the English make most intensive use of their grounds. They invariably divide them, no matter how small they may be, into little parcels with well established boundaries. It is this custom Americanized that is the subject of this problem.

The ground in front of the house is developed into a shrub and tree bounded lawn, kept very simple to be in keeping with the informal and semi-suburban character of a Fall River street. The planting along the sidewalk is high enough so that you can stand unnoticed on the lawn but it is low enough to allow from the entrance porch a view of the Fall River harbor. This view is a valuable asset to the property, for on the sloping land, just across the street, steel gray rock ledges are overgrown with Bayberry, Sweet Fern, and wild Roses, while below is the harbor, and beyond it the checker-board particolored fields of Rhode Island framed in by the low hills of Connecticut, all blue and gray in the distance. The omission of the planting along the street would have given a broader and barer view of the harbor but this more restricted outlook through the leafy frame of shrubs and arching elm branches is far more pleasing.

For the lawn enclosure it is essential to plant not only boundary plantations but borders along the house. This is often a difficult problem. The composition of such a shrubbery, while interesting in itself, must be in keeping with the house. It is necessary to take into account, also, the window arrangement so that spreading branches will not encroach upon it. This difficulty was eliminated here. The balustraded unroofed porch, resembling a terrace, allows the use of a continuous shrubbery border, but even then, it is necessary to see that the shrubbery is not allowed to grow too thick and massive.

The ground in back of the house is divided into four parts. Through the center of the lot runs a flower-bordered path. This terminates in the vegetable garden. Relegated to the north side of the lot, to be near the kitchen, are laundry yard, garage, auto run and turn-around arranged in a closely related and efficient group. On the south side is a small rectangle enclosed by shrubbery which is called the orchard because of its five dwarf fruit trees. Enclosed by vine-covered fences, lattice screens, free-growing shrubbery, and clipped hedges, each subdivision can be treated as a part by itself and can concentrate upon itself all the interest of the moment.

The garage is connected with the house. Many interesting problems in house building and in the development of the grounds would arise from a desire of weaving house and garage into one architectural composition. It would do away with the many and for the most part ugly little outbuildings which are spoiling many small suburban properties.

The laundry yard is a narrow space between the garage and the lattice screen of the garden. The auto run with an exit on a back street is a pleasant tunnel under trees that arch overhead. The turn-around is bounded by hedges and by high fences completely hidden under rampant Honeysuckle vines. The orchard is enclosed by shrubbery. The shrubs are planted in straight rows but the difference in their habits of growth and in the spread of their branches gives the appearance of an irregular plantation.

The flower garden consists of narrow flower beds bordering a brick path. It is the very simplest kind of flower garden. The lattice on the north side and the hedge on the south side form backgrounds which will in time make it a secluded walk. It is one of the prime requisites of small perennial borders that they be crowded with plants. In a very small garden it is well to remember several points in making a choice of flowers. Plants should be chosen for their foliage effectiveness. They should be selected for striking flowers so that a few plants will make strong color notes in the planting. Plants with long blooming periods should be given preference, for then only a few kinds will be needed for a continuous effect. When the backbone of the border has been thus established, then many other plants can be inserted for added color interest. The path, however, does not end with the flower borders. Beyond the rose arch it extends between hedges of Currant bushes to the end of the property. This change in the borders of the path seems to increase the length of the vista and gives a feeling of extent to the grounds. The vista is to be terminated by a garden seat harmonious in design with the lattice which is to be placed in front of a narrow border of shrubs, growing in the shade of several Maples.

The property has a homey quality. It is developed in a logical, straightforward way in direct response to practical needs. Its plan is definite, clear cut, and compact. Each and every part has been given its appropriate share of plant beauty. For these reasons it ought to be suggestive for other lots of small size.

PROBLEM VII

A Simple Home-Ground on a Small Wooded Hillside, by Warren H. Manning, Landscape Designer, Boston, Mass.

This property is located at Newark, N. J. Its dimensions are 100 x 275 feet

A SHRUBBERY - BOUNDED lawn, a flower garden, a woods with a curving drive are some of the understood requisites of a large estate, but to have all three of them in the suburbs on a steeply sloping lot of only a 100 feet frontage and 275 feet depth hardly seems possible until we see a concrete example such as this.

Its simplicity, dignity, and naturalness distinguish it from all the thoughtless and unfinished planting of neighboring lots and shows that efficient treatment and organized planning is as necessary for a small place as for a large one. This lot is fortunate in having some tall trees with a mass of undergrowth characteristic of deciduous woods.

The house is well placed, back from the street, and has a fine suburban spirit. It is low and rambling with quaint roof lines that make it nestle among the trees.

The plan as here produced is of the place as it appeared at the time when the chapter was first written and not wholly as it was originally planned. The plan was left in the hands of the owner to carry out. Certain things were changed, by the owner's own confession, not always to its advantage, certain things have never been developed in accordance with the original intent, but the touch of the landscape architect's hand is on it.

In the making of the garden picture, there are two duties to be performed, a duty to outsiders and a duty to oneself. The planting, like the exterior of the house, ought to be an asset to the street; the grounds, like the interior of the house, ought to be primarily for one's own comfort and enjoyment, a place as private as possible so that it can be in reality an out-of-door room. Here a Barberry hedge is planted along the front. The simple break in the hedge at the entrance steps with their edging of trailing *Rosa wichuriana* is more appropriate than gate posts or any other

Problem VII.

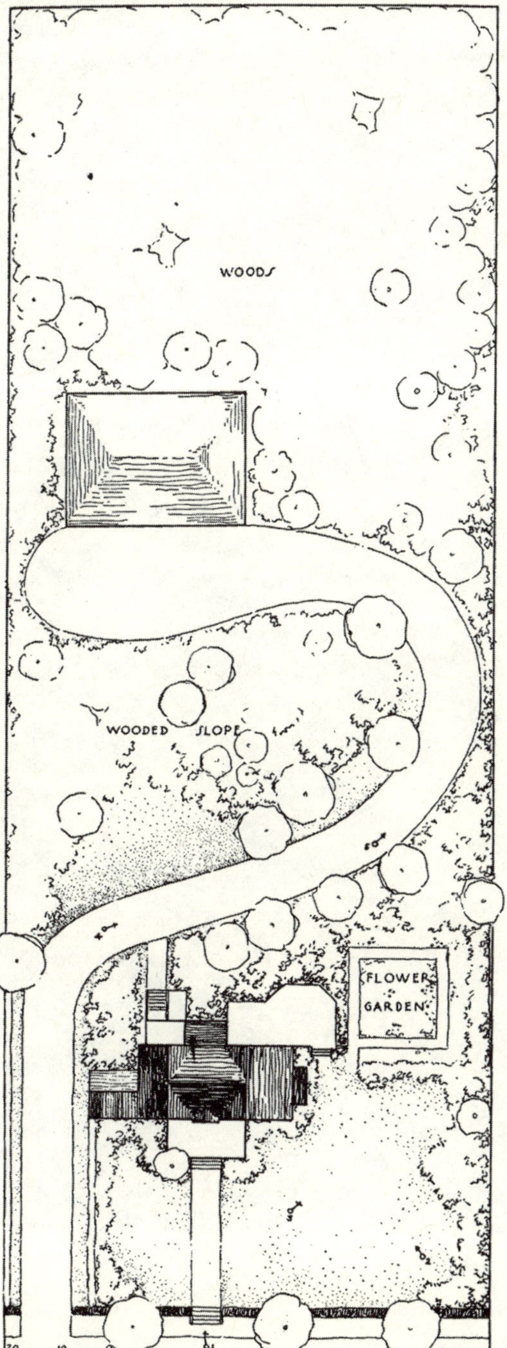

The Plan.

Problem VII. No. 1.

The Street View.

form of emphasis could have been. The Barberry has an informality of habit well suited to this house. When left unclipped, as it is here, it has a spreading habit which is very pleasing for its position here on the top of the low grass terrace. Hedge and terrace together form a barrier of six or seven feet which gives just enough privacy to the front lawn without making it too exclusive, for, as you look over it from the street, you can see the Lilac tree near the porch and the Wistaria on the corner of the house, and glimpses of the shrubs in the borders.

The first impression you get, once inside the hedge, is a feeling of space: for though the front lawn is not more than 80 feet in width and about 40 feet in depth it is smooth and uninterrupted. There is, however, no picture in just a green lawn. The surrounding line of trees and shrubbery is the source of its beauty; it gives to it the color of the flowers and the varying green of foliage, and the changing shadows. Here the street trees enter into the scheme for they supply the large trees without encroaching upon the lawn space.

The planting along the house foundations is an interesting use of low growing plants with taller shrubs and vines and small trees. It is the purpose of the small shrubs to soften the fixed rectangular lines of the house with gracefully curving and spreading branches, to nestle close to the foundations, and be a link between the house wall and the lawn. The shrubs are planted closely together to give continuous effect of foliage in summer and of twigs and branches in winter. The use of one kind of plant would be monotonous, the use of too many kinds spotty, not only in flower effect but in foliage values. *Spiræa thunbergii* and *Stephanandra flexuosa* are planted along the front of the house, an Actinidia vine tumbles luxuriantly over the porch railing, a Wistaria climbs up the corner of the house, and climbing Roses and Peonies are planted under the south window. Together, they form an intermittent succession of bloom from late April to late June.

Lilacs are used to form the high part of the south shrubbery and are the main feature of it. A predominance of one kind of shrub, especially in so small a border, is one way of insuring a harmonious foliage effect and of avoiding a spotty effect. With two kinds of Forsythia, Rugosa Roses, and Snowberries, the bloom lasts from April until August. Though the house shrubbery and

At the Side of the House.

Problem VII. No. 3.

The Lawn.

that of the border are each complete in themselves, they complement one another. The Spiræa and Forsythia give a white and yellow effect which is bright and cheerful in early spring, later the Wistaria and Lilacs give a quieter effect of lavender and purple.

Naturally the emphasis of the lawn planting was centered on the south side as it is seen from the main living room. Through this concentration, the north side was neglected. The original plan calls for a low wall on either side of the drive and for shrubbery on the north side of the lawn. It is so indicated on the plan here presented to show how such treatment would hide the drive from the front lawn and complete the picture of the lawn with its surrounding trees and flowering shrubbery.

The small flower garden, which divides the front lawn from the woods in the back, is well placed on the side of the piazza. Besides the shrubbery bounding it on the front and the woods in the back, a trellis for vines on the side opposite the piazza hides it from the neighbor's kitchen. The charm of many a flower garden is due to its bounding lines and these are possible in the smallest garden.

A flower garden is not an absolute necessity for

a well arranged informally planted small place. It can be considered as its luxury. It has not been made much of in this place. The space left for it is really very small, far too small for a regular garden, but such a little square can be crowded with flowers, leaving only enough room for the very narrow paths necessary to tend them. The plants want to be placed very close together in order to cover the entire space. They want to make a closely woven color pattern, for, sitting on the piazza or standing by the railing, you get a bird's-eye view looking down into the bloom. Such a secluded little spot need not be kept in fine trim, nor can it be kept in continuous bloom. It seems best to limit the bloom to one season and to get one fine effect. It could be primarily a spring garden with Daffodils or late Tulips with early ground covers like creeping Phloxes, or it could become a lovely tangle of Irises and Yellow Day Lilies, it could be quite a choice little spot filled with several kinds of white Lilies, or it could become an autumn garden full of perennial Asters or hardy Chrysanthemums.

In back of the house, the ground drops off at a very steep grade. Many people avoid such steep properties. They do not see any possibility of

The Glade.

The Drive through the Woods.

making them attractive and let them grow up rank with weeds and washed into gullies for it is well-nigh impossible to make them into lawns. Such slopes are not easy to handle but their very difficulties encourage their opportunities. It is interesting, for instance, to transform them into little woodlands. Such treatment is especially harmonious with a low informal picturesque house such as this one. Even if the ground is devoid of trees, a woods effect can be created in a comparatively short period of time through the planting of some extra sized trees and a thick naturalistic planting of wild shrubs and small trees. On this lot, it was not a problem of creating a woods for the slope was part of a century-old forest, it was the problem of preserving the character and spirit of the woods through the planting of shade-loving shrubs and woodsy flowers. The owner realized and appreciated his opportunity and though it could be improved through more and better planting, the enchantment of the woods has been preserved in wonderful contrast to the neighbor's yard where the trees have been destroyed.

The road is a frank straightforward piece of engineering to get from the street level to the barn at a grade possible for a horse. The curve is a little steep for the automobile, which came into use after the road was built, but it is not impracticable except in very slippery winter weather. The road's very picturesqueness is due to the curve which was a necessity. It provides a series of woodland pictures. The views from the dining room windows and from the piazza are especially charming. The open glade where the road runs along the back of the house provides a small laundry yard.

Trees and shrubs, for the most part deciduous, predominate over flowers and ever-greens. These give interest to the grounds in all seasons. In spring they cheer with delicate flowers, in summer they rest with abundant green and shade, in autumn and winter they enliven the grounds with bright fruit and colored twigs. This is one of the most important points to keep in mind in the planting of small places, for the suburban grounds are the setting for houses which are in use the year around.[1]

[1] Since the chapter was written and the pictures taken, the original owner has died and the place has been sold. Through neglect and changes made by an untutored and unsympathetic hand the place has almost lost in the short space of two years its essential charm. The place never had unusual care, nor did it require the trimness of less informal places, but now it has lost the ever sympathetic understanding of its spirit. I make note of it with regret in justice to the original owner and to the landscape architect, to emphasize the worth of intelligent maintenance.

PROBLEM VIII

An Informal Arrangement of a Small Property, by Harold A. Caparn, Landscape Architect, New York City

This property is located at Larchmont, N. Y. Its dimensions are 150 x 200 feet

THIS oblong piece of land, less than an acre, lies between the street and a picturesque inlet of Long Island Sound. An outcrop of rock formed the highest part of the ground, which sloped first gently, then with an abrupt dip toward the water. A few old Apple trees were dotted along its outlines, old overgrown and intergrown Thorns were scattered about in big groups. Such were the existing conditions.

The house is located on a rocky ledge. The stone of the cellar excavation was used for the building of the first story. The ledge as an integral part of the house, together with the Thorns which are by merest chance so picturesquely grouped around it, suggested the name of "Thornledge."

The house stands very near the street boundary which is an advantage as it allows an uninterrupted use of the grounds. On a small property this fact is particularly worthy of note. There would have been no advantage in setting the house back from the village street, which has no traffic, while it was very desirable to get a big expanse of lawn as a foreground for the inlet view. As this is on the southern side of the house it was important, too, to place the main rooms upon it. This seems the most logical development, a natural solution, the only one in fact, yet you will find that very few people take such important matters into consideration in house building. This same care is shown in placing the house parallel to the stream at the foot of the property and caused its unusual angle to the street which is not noticeable at all because of the ingenious arrangement of the entrance with the inset of the gate on the diagonal. Inside the gate, the shrubbery, the curve of the brick walk, and the tangle of Thorns hide the front door. The Carmine Pillar Roses and Clematis on the gate arch, the Rhododendrons along the house wall, the Laurels around the front porch,

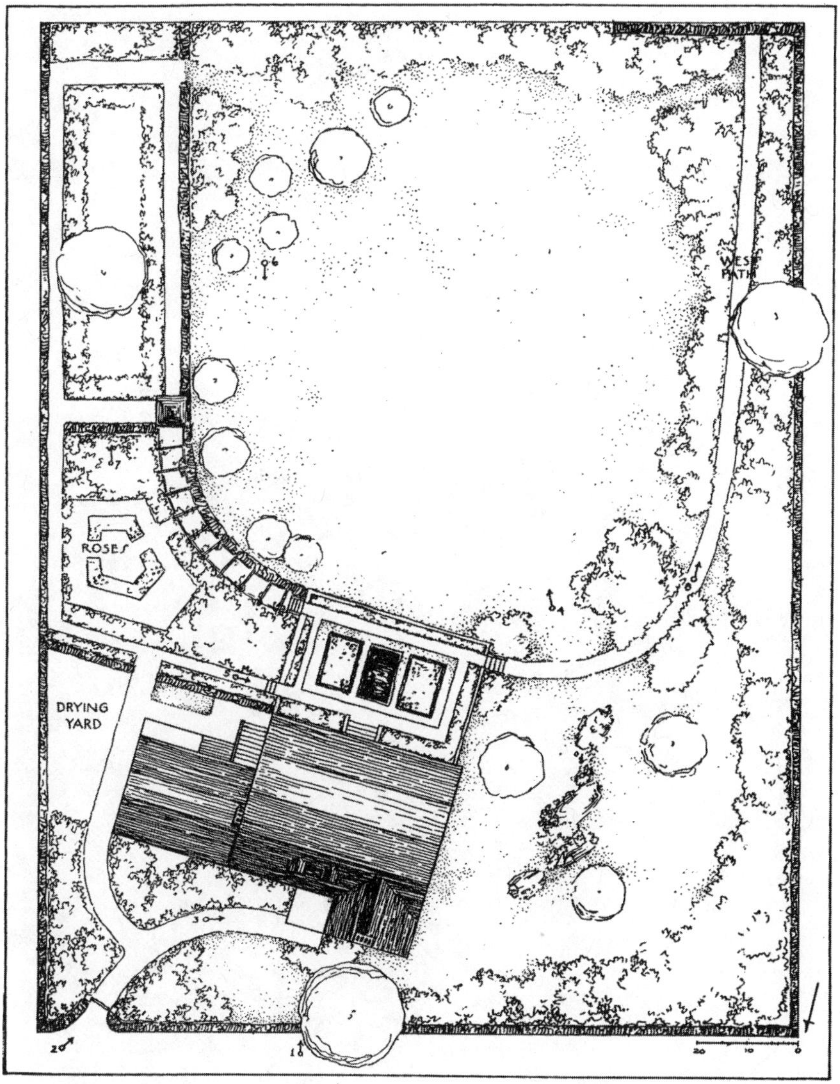

The Plan.

Problem VIII. No. 1.

The Street View.

the Thorns along the walk, the Apple tree near the hedge, the shrubs grouped in a heavy mass along the side boundary combine in giving continuous interest and color to the entrance walk and emphasize the informal character of the house.

Service paths on small properties are especially difficult problems to deal with. The monotony in so many suburban and city streets where two straight paths cut up each lot front and form tiresome ribbon bands of paving along the whole street makes any ingenuity and originality expressed in the solving of this problem welcome. Here, it seems most naturally done. The little branch path curves off the main path and then it is almost hidden by the outstretching branches of the shrubbery borders. It has the essential demanded of all the service parts of the grounds, that they are screened and hidden away from all the rest of the property.

Tree and shrub enclosures are absolute essentials in developing lawns. What they add to the lawn, in giving privacy and in creating general interest, is not generally appreciated nor understood by owners of small properties. For the surroundings of most lawns the boundaries should be as high and heavy and impregnable as tall trees and shrubbery can make them. The same trees and shrubbery that here bound the lawn space hide the barn buildings on neighboring properties and make a frame for the view.

This property is only 150 by 200 feet. For the complete and intensive use of a piece of ground, even of this size, more than a lawn is necessary.

A terrace is a means of transition between the house and lawn. Terraces are capable of many forms, shapes, and characters. They can be spacious, dignified, ornate, and formal to harmonize with the most elaborate house, they can be as small, simple, and informal as any suburban house may require. Here the small oblong grass plot is surrounded by narrow brick paths which are bounded on the outer side by unclipped Barberry hedging. This is the simplest form a terrace can take. It is particularly fortunate in winter to have such a sunny spot close to the house. The brick paths make it dry to walk on and the red Barberry berries look bright and cheery. In the first plan for the terrace the grass plot was divided into three panels, a pool in the center with flowers on either side. This idea, shown on the

Problem VIII. No. 2.

The Entrance Gate.

Problem VIII. No. 3.

The Entrance Porch.

Problem VIII. No. 4.

The Lawn.

plan, illustrates how even such a small place can be full of interest and color.

Steps from the terrace lead down to narrow strips of ground on the east and west sides of the lawn. The eastern side of the property was originally thought out as the service side of the garden but it is so full of color and flowers that it hardly gives any suggestion of the original intention. A path runs along the whole length to a tool house. It is shut off from the lawn by a hedge and for part of the way it is under the curving grape arbor. It is very simply built, its curve is interesting, and its pointed roof construction gives a rather quaint impression. It is built very low and is set so far below the terrace that in a very few years it has become almost hidden by the maturing trees, shrubbery, and vines.

On the side of the arbor is an oddly shaped little piece of ground given to Roses and small fruits. Many kinds of native and bush Roses are planted in a thick mass along the terrace wall. *Rosa Blanda*, *Rosa spinossissima*, Persian Yellow Roses, *Rosa rubrifolia*, *Rosa rubiginosa* which is the Sweet Brier, *Rosa nitida*, *Rosa lucida*, Madam Pantier Roses, and *Rosa carolina*, to attempt to give them in their succession of bloom, give a bright tangle of color.

Every garden should have Roses for cutting and yet Hybrid Tea and Hybrid Perpetual Roses can hardly be associated with shrubbery. It is difficult to find an appropriate place for them in a garden which is developed in such a naturalistic way as this one. Here, they have been planted in beds with the Gooseberries and Currants. This arrangement gives both Roses and small fruits the space they need for good development. If Roses cannot have the dignity of a separate garden, which is hardly possible in a small place of this kind where intensive use ought to be made of every bit of ground, this combination of Roses and small fruits is a very good one.

To the north of the Roses is the drying yard tucked away behind hedges. Iris and Chrysanthemums are planted along the side of the hedge. To the south of the Roses is an oblong plot originally planned for the vegetable garden, but now a secluded little nook. The great old Apple tree makes it a nice shady little spot with the simple lawn space between yellow Iris that grow on one side and white and pink Peonies on the other.

While the eastern side of the property is allotted to utilitarian purposes and shows how pretty such a

The Terrace.

The Pergola.

useful little strip of ground can be made, the west side was developed in a purely decorative way

The outcropping ledges immediately to the west of the house are overgrown with Wichuriana Roses and in among them are such rock plants as the yellow Sedums and creeping Phloxes and Helianthemum which form a wild little spot almost entirely enclosed yet a part of the larger lawn.

The west path starts at the terrace and makes a big generous curve to the extreme western side of the grounds. It is an informal one passing through masses of shrubbery. Interspersed with the shrubs to brighten them with color spots and fill in bare places are patches of low and creeping flowers which grow over the rough stone edging of the path. Occasionally the shrub mass is broken, just enough to give views of the lawn through the gaps.

Such paths, full of interest in growing and flowering things, are ways of making the grounds seem larger. There is no attempt at deception or optical delusion. The result is gained simply by engrossing one's interest in every step of the way so that one lingers longer upon it. A curved path is better for this than a straight one. The curved path gradually unfolds its varied pictures to the beholder as he passes along while a straight path opens up one long vista to him all at one time. The planting of a straight path needs to be arranged to obtain one unified effect throughout its entire length, the planting of a curving path, where only little portions of the way are seen, can be made up of a series of different effects. Such a path can be kept continually interesting, not only one part of it but along its whole course. This interest is obtained not through great diversity of plants but through thoughtful distribution. Each group of plants—for a border in plan is divided into arbitrary groups not visible in the planting—is composed of two or three kinds of shrubs that arouse attention at different times. Japanese Barberry and *Clethra alnifolia*, the Sweet Pepper Bush, are interplanted. The Japanese Barberry provides early spring bloom and winter interest and the Sweet Pepper Bush gives a good summer effect with its white flowers. *Spiræa Anthony Waterer* and *Hypericum aureum* have two different summer periods of bloom. *Kerria japonica* and Snowberries have two periods. The white Snowberries are effective in autumn and the green Kerria stems are conspicuous in winter time. *Cornus*

The Apple Tree.

The Shrubbery Path.

alba and Common Barberry are interplanted. The Barberry has its greenish yellow pendants in April, the Cornel has small flat clusters of white flowers in June. In autumn the white Cornel berries make a contrast with the red fruit of the Barberry and in winter *Cornus alba* has brilliant red stems. Again Stephanandra and Regel's Privet are planted together. One blooms in May, the other in July. They have an interesting winter effectiveness for the Stephanandra stems are orange tinted and the Privet has persistent black fruit. *Philadelphus microphyllus* and *Spiræa Anthony Waterer* are grouped together. The foliage delicacy and small dainty white flowers of this variety of Mock Orange are quite choice in comparison with the coarser growth of the Spiræa and give two distinctly different effects to the same spot.

In such careful massing the shrubs can be used in small groups, sometimes only one of a kind, sometimes five or six plants used together. In this kind of grouping there is always something new and interesting, always something different on the path to attract attention, through the whole cycle of seasons, which makes a new little garden adventure every time we pass along.

While the attention given to seasonal effects makes this path of continual interest, it is the consideration given to the foliage effect and to shrub habit which binds the shrubs together into a unified border. It is the complexity of these varied considerations that makes border planting such a difficult problem, one which requires an artistic feeling to do it justice.

PROBLEM IX

A Formal Arrangement of a Suburban Property, by Oglesby Paul, Landscape Architect

This property is located at Villa Nova, Pa. Its dimensions are 150 x 300 feet

THIS garden reminds me of a triptych of an old altarpiece for it is made up of three parts built upon straight lines in a carefully balanced design. The main picture is in the large central panel while the narrow wings picture the minor events. The central garden is in full view of the house. It is the garden which is most carefully tended and in it the succession of bloom is carefully carried out. The side gardens, as the lesser parts of the design, are reserved for special effects. They are more secluded, more sheltered, and therefore need less careful attention.

One often imagines that only a large place can support such a set of gardens but they have been compacted into this small area with great nicety.

Each part has a feeling of breadth and bigness, for the design is worked out on simple and straightforward lines.

The house has a simple plan. The front and back of the main portion are very similar with a central doorway flanked on both sides by two windows. To one side of the main portion is the porch, on the other side the service wing.

The central doorway encourages the balanced design of the gardens as it necessitates a strong axis line. Upon it are arranged three interestingly varied parts. Just outside the door is a little courtlike place. It is hedged with clipped Privet and paved with old brick laid herringbone. Pyramidal Box bushes flank the doorway and Hollyhocks are growing up by the side of the windows. On either side are very simple wooden benches and in back of each stands a standard globe-shaped Privet. These clipped curiosities are becoming very common in nurseries and are being very much misused and overused. It is safest to avoid them altogether. Occasionally, however, such oddities have a place in strictly formal positions as in this little hedged off place near the house. Outside the hedge—still centered

Problem IX.

The Plan.

The House.

on the main axis—the octagonal pool ornamented with four clipped Box balls stands in the center of a little *piazza*. Beyond the pool is the lawn which is the central picture of the triptych. Old Apple and Pear trees, that have roses climbing up the trunks, are scattered over it and give it a quaint old-fashioned look. The lawn is edged on its four sides by flower borders. When I first saw these borders, early in June, they were mainly blue and white with touches of cream and pink. There were clumps of Iris and groups of Lupines at more or less regular intervals with Columbines scattered in between. I saw them again the last of June. Then the Madonna Lilies were out in great numbers. Larkspurs were sprinkled through the borders in delicate groups and pink Sweet William was out, making almost too thick a mat.

At the farther end of the lawn a wall extends across the whole width of the property. The old-time spirit of the garden is expressed best perhaps in this wall with its gray cement finish, its brick coping, its vines—Actinidia and Grape, Honeysuckle and Roses—that are making a tangle over it. This same quaintness is accentuated in its architectural features. At one end is an arched opening with lattice bars. The recessed seat, in the center, has a slightly curved arch overhead and a delicate lattice back on which Roses are clambering. Next to it is a round-headed gateway with a solid wooden door. At the other end is the best of all its features, a curved seat forming a segment of a circle. The lattice at its back is arranged in panels that look like casement windows and above it there is a beamed overhang. Something about this seat, placed in the deep shade of tall trees with only faint mottled sunlight coming down through the leaves, something in its cool gray, almost ruined look gives it a charming timeworn spirit. Such a feeling in a ten-year-old garden is not the result of neglect but is expressive of an indescribable atmosphere which is found in gardens where there is a leaving of well enough alone.

The side panels of the triptych are composed of long straight grass paths. One is bordered by deciduous shrubbery and flowers, the other by evergreens. Such straight paths have a host of possibilities. In England the lovely wall gardens and clipped Yew walks are built along straight lines. In the south we have remnants of Box-edged paths

Problem IX. No. 2.

The Pergola.

Problem IX. No. 3.

The Pool.

PROBLEM IX. NO. 4.

THE LAWN.

PROBLEM IX. NO. 5.

THE SEAT IN THE WALL.

and alleys of old trees. Grass walks bordered by free-growing shrubbery and trees with all the interest which comes from varying foliage tones and interesting skylines make possible a host of fine possibilities for modern gardens. Here the deciduous shrubbery path is a very shady one. The trees arch overhead and the shrubbery spreads its branches over the grass. The prevailing lines are horizontal. The evergreen path has just the same dimensions but the columnar habit of the trees keeps the path open to the sky and the dominant lines perpendicular.

When shrubbery plays the dominant part in the border, as it does in this deciduous shrubbery path, it is difficult to incorporate flowers into it. I have seen so many instances where flowers add only fussy little farcical parts to really good shrubbery acting. This failing in flowers to play their legitimate part is very noticeable in paths of this kind where they must be treated frankly as subordinates and yet where they have a chance to heighten the interest by some really clever touches. What attracted me to this path was the chance glimpse—over the neighbor's hedge—when the Oriental Poppies were blooming. Scattered singly at regular intervals throughout the length of both borders their strong color was silhouetted against the green of grass and shrub. It is the use of this rich color all alone amid the green which makes the very uniformity of the effect so splendid. When such single effects follow one another month by month, the flower succession is quite wonderful.

In selecting flowers for such individual effects in connection with shrubbery, great care ought to be taken to make the plants really count. Plants with vivid coloring like Lychnis, Orange Milkweed, and Tiger Lilies are good; plants with a shrubby habit like *Baptista australis*, the Blue Indigo, and *Buddlea variabilis*, the Butterfly Flower, and *Careopteris mastacanthus*, the Blue Spiræa, are excellent; and plants that adapt themselves easily to naturalization like Daffodils and Mertensias, like Meadow Rues and Snakeroots, like Asters and Joe Pye Weed and Goldenrods, are very effective.

In the borders of the evergreen walk, the perpendicular lines are gained through the use of Retinisporas. The emphasis upon this one variety gives the path a satisfying stability while the few Pines and Hemlocks that are scattered at the back of the borders relieve the possibility of any monotony. I had hitherto considered that Retini-

Problem IX. No. 6.

The Shrubbery Path.

Problem IX. No. 7.

The Evergreen Path.

The Gate in the Wall.

sporas were only good for strictly formal effects, but here by being scattered along the length of the borders in irregularly placed groups of two or three plants they have attained a distinctly informal feeling. They have been so grouped that in each small clump plants of different tints and different feathered foliage offset one another, which gives variety in foliage and a nice warmth of tone to the borders.

Azalea amœna and *Abelia rupestris* form the predominent note among the lower plants that are used between the Retinispora groups. The foliage of these two varieties is so harmonious that they look charming so interplanted. The spreading habit and lovely foliage of the *Azalea amœna* make it a welcomed member of a border in summer and in winter but its magenta flowers are a difficult color element to deal with in most places. Here, however, where it is the only color at the time it is in bloom amid many evergreens, its brightness must be altogether pleasing and refreshing. While the *Azalea amœna* makes the important spring color, the *Abelia rupestris* gives a charmingly soft effect with pale blush flowers in drooping clusters in early autumn. In between the Azalea and Abelia groups are scattered other plants that give foliage variety without disturbing the unity of the borders. Here is a plant of gray-toned *Juniperus pfitzerii*, there a few *Pinus mugho*, here a Yew, there a bush of unclipped Box, here a few Dogwoods for a spring touch, there one Elder for June, and farther on a dwarf Horse-Chestnut for July and August, and most charming of all a flame-colored Ghent Azalea blooming beside a lavender Rhododendron in early June. This exquisite color study is at the end of the evergreen path in front of the semicircular seat. As it can be seen from across the big central garden it is particularly lovely when it helps to key up the blue of the Iris and Lupines that are blooming at that time. These paintable bits linger long in one's memory.[1]

[1] I obtained permission from Mr. Oglesby Paul to make use of this problem some months before his death. Paul and Ford, his successors, have been very kind in putting the plan at my disposal.

PROBLEM X

A Naturalistic Arrangement of a City Property, by Alling S. DeForest, Landscape Architect, Rochester, N. Y.

This property is located at Rochester, N. Y. Its dimensions are 120 x 500 feet

THE elongated proportions of this city lot, with the unusual depth of 500 feet, gave the opportunity for the naturalistic development of this property. The main interest is centered upon the big South lawn in back of the house. It is a long, sunny grass space bounded by heavy enclosures. Behind it is a smaller lawn, more secluded and wilder for the Narcissus that are naturalized in the grass prevent its mowing until the leaves have died down. Tucked away in one corner beside the Narcissus lawn is the Wild garden. South lawn, Narcissus lawn, and Wild garden are connected by a curving path. This path affords an easy short cut from the house to a farther street on which the car line is located and gives a pleasant opportunity for the daily use of the property.

On one side of the South lawn, on the east side of the property, are the drive, service court, and garage. They have been put there to be near the kitchen and out of the view of the living room windows and the porches. This seems such a logical arrangement that it is difficult to understand the possibilities of any other, and yet in the scheme first arranged before the landscape architect's services were solicited, the drive swung around the back of the house and ended in a turn-around and garage at the west side of the property directly in back of the living rooms. A hard gravel strip of drive would have divided the house from the entire back of the property and garage and turn-around enclosure would have hidden it away from view. It was to have been a sorry prosaic place full of the cares of a household. It needed a bigger vision to relegate all the service to the kitchen side of the house and in that way preserve an unbroken lawn which could be enclosed by quiet foliage, enlivened by the color of flowers, and made pleasant by the play of shadows on the grass. It needed an imagination to create this

Problem X.

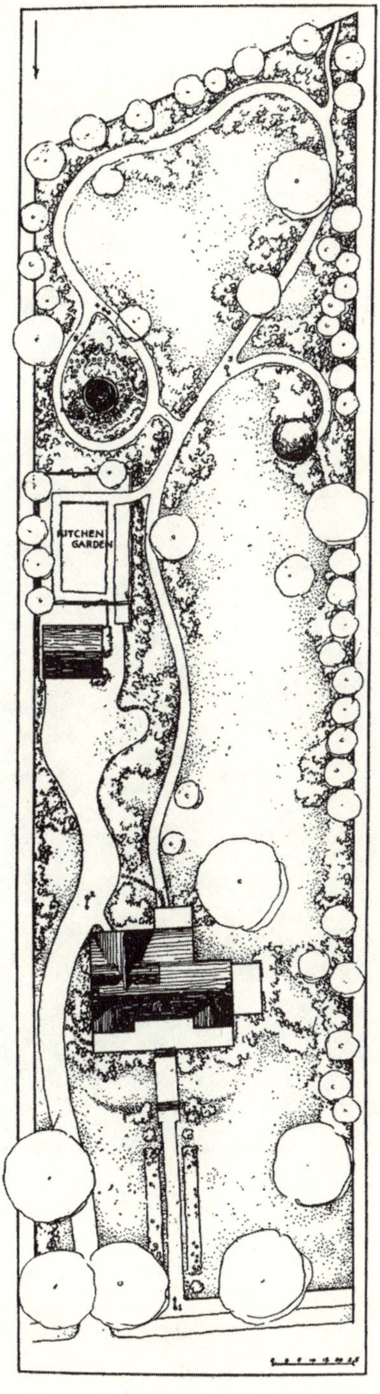

The Plan.

The Entrance Path.

lawn which was to foster through a diminutive and freely rendered replica of natural scenes a delight in the wide out-of-doors by putting the lawn where it could be seen directly from the windows of the living rooms, by making it an easy matter to step right out on the grass, and by tempting one through interesting plant material to explore all the nooks and corners of lawn and garden.

The emphasis of the planting of the South lawn is laid on the west boundary. Such boundary screens are generally considered by the layman as a collection of heterogeneous shrub and tree material planted close together without much thought as to arrangement. This unfortunate and erroneous idea may be dispelled by a careful analysis of this screen plantation. It may show that it is an artistic problem, that the assemblage of trees, shrubs, and flowers into a good border requires not merely a horticultural understanding of individual plants but an artistic perception of how they will look when united into a border. This west boundary is a composition of contrasts. Big masses of large trees and tall shrubbery curve boldly out into the lawn, making strong promontories and leaving in between bays bordered by a shallow planting of small trees and low shrubbery. There are four such promontories. The first, beside the house, is made of Hemlocks and White Pines with an undergrowth of native and hybrid Rhododendrons. This is a strong group of more than fifty plants. The second promontory is composed of *Pinus sylvestris*, the Scotch Pine, and a group of twenty flowering Dogwood trees. In spring the wonderful white bracts of the Dogwood flowers find a foil in the green of the pine, and in the autumn the evergreens make a background for the Dogwoods' striking red foliage and bright fruit. The third promontory is a slight one but marked by three *Abies concolor*. These *Abies concolor* or White Firs, which like the Blue Spruce have been very greatly misused as lawn decorations—lawn disfigurements—have gained a charming place for themselves here. Plants of such unusual color enliven the border. They must be used only where they will not spoil the color effect of other plants. They must be used only in an extensive border, and even then only very sparingly. The fourth promontory is the strongest part of the boundary. It marks the end of the South lawn and furnishes a background for the rustic shelter. The columnar Cedars and Arbor Vitæs in the foreground make striking

The Service Drive.

The South Lawn.

contrasts with the sturdy bushy White Pines in back of them. A feathery Larch is planted in this group, a few *Juniperus glauca* with grayish foliage are placed with the Arbor Vitæs, and spring flowering Spiræas, *S. van houttei*, *S. reevsii*, and *S. rotundifolia*, make interesting contrasts of white flowers against the Cedars.

Between these promontories are shrubberies with a background of flowering trees. The various Magnolias, the native Thorns, Dogwoods, and Fringe Trees give a succession of spring bloom. The cup-shaped Magnolia flowers, the abundant clusters of small Hawthorn blossoms, the large bracts of the Dogwood, and the great white panicles of the Fringe Tree each have a striking and distinctive character. The shrubberies of the bays start with *Lonicera fragrantissima*, the Fragrant Bush Honeysuckle, with very early April blossoms. Next to them is a bold mass of Peonies. These and the hybrid Rhododendrons blooming at the same time make a wonderfully rich display in June. Near the Dogwoods the flat branched *Viburnum tomentosum*, the single Japanese Snowball, and the cut-leaved Sumac, *Rhus glabra lacinata*, make an effective contrast. Farther on Barberries have a value near *Pinus mugho* and dwarf Arbor Vitæ.

Plants with delicate leafage like the cut-leaved Sumac, or of striking structure like the *Viburnum tomentosum*, plants with unusual shapes like the round-headed *Pinus mugho* (which is wonderfully effective when it grows old and loose branched) or distinctive character like the Cedars, have a value in varying the appearance of the boundary and in that way prolonging the interest in the border. The character of individual plants must not be overemphasized at the expense of spoiling the continuity of the plantation. Therefore, the matter of choosing the proper proportion of each kind of plant is one of delicacy.

There is, too, a succession of interesting seasonal effects. The border changes in appearance almost every week in a kind of magical sequence as flowers appear one after another, as foliage develops and turns to bright colors and berries mature. And even in the winter every shrub and tree exhibits a distinctive character displayed in structure, color of branches and fruit. Besides, the blending of this deciduous material with evergreens gives charming effects to the winter lawn.

The Narcissus lawn has a character quite distinct from the South lawn. The differentiation is obtained through the use of other plant material arranged with a different idea in mind. The shrubbery between the path and the lawn is composed of all kinds of shrubs that are rich in flowering effects. On the other side of the path, in the boundary plantation, shrubs with interesting fruit and winter color predominate. The border starts with *Aralia spinosa.* Its host of black berries follow immediately after great panicles of white flowers. Next is a great mass of Privet with black winter berries and *Eleagnus augustifolia* with silvery fruit. Then come *Viburnum tomentosum*, *Viburnum lentago*, and *Viburnum opulus* with striking large white flower clusters and wonderful autumn foliage and red fruit. The Bush Honeysuckles, which are interplanted with them, produce delicate translucent berries, some yellow, some orange, some red, which mature early in July. Next are groups of Indian Currants and Snowberries. They are small graceful shrubs but inconspicuous until the fall brings forth their interesting berries, one coral red in heavy clusters on drooping branches, the other round and white on long pendants. Next comes Rhamnus or Buckthorn, a garden favorite of a hundred years ago with shining black fruit, then the

Common Barberry with scarlet berries, then *Ilex verticillata* or Winterberry. This is a very modest, retiring plant until winter arrives and then its small berries clinging close to the stem are the most brilliant of all the winter fruits. On the east boundary are Yellowroot with interesting autumn foliage, the black-berried Elders, a July fruiting shrub, and *Cornus stolonifera* with conspicuous red stems during the winter time. This collection of berry-bearing shrubs produces color effects which make a wonderful winter garden quite independent of evergreens.

The Wild garden has an individual character of its own. The bowlder-edged pond has given an incentive to use water-loving plants, plants of a rock garden character, and such as will make good pictures when reflected in the water. In the pond Water Lilies are growing. Immediately on the edge are Azaleas in vivid scarlet, yellow, and orange tints. There are also groups of Japanese Iris, Yellow Day Lilies, and ornamental grasses. All these have interesting sheathlike foliage appropriate at the water's edge. On the other side of the stepping-stone path which bounds this planting, Cedars are planted in a mass just as they grow

The Path between the Lawn and the Wild Garden.

The Wild Garden.

naturally on hillsides. The ground between them is covered with all kinds of rock plants, white Rock Cress, dark violet Aubretia, snowy Candytuft, white *Cerastium tomentosum*, and blue *Phlox divaricata*. They flower throughout the spring and afterwards their varied foliage, the gray tufts of Arabis, the silvery tone of Cerastium, the dark leaves of Candytuft, the gray of Aubretia, are as interesting as the flowers. A few Yuccas are interspersed with the Cedars for midsummer effect. In back of them, Roses are planted. There are lovely *Rosa spinossissima*, *Rosa multiflora*, and *Rosa setigera* with long arching branches, and *Rosa wichuriana* which covers the ground with long streamers. In early summer the wealth of single pink and white flowers is offset by the dark green of Cedars; in winter they are again a decorative feature when the rose hips are contrasted against the evergreens.

The charm of this place depends upon the distinct individuality of each subdivision, upon its interesting diversity of shape, character, and plant material, and upon the unifying informality of the design.

PROBLEM XI

A Naturalistic Garden—A Study in Flower Color, by Marian C. Coffin, Landscape Architect, New York City

This property is located at Flushing, N. Y. Its dimensions are 150 x 300 feet

IN this small place the interest is so concentrated upon the flowers that it seems like one big flower garden. From the back porch we can look down the Peony path to the wide stretched Iris borders and across them to the herbaceous borders that encircle the big lawn.

On either side of the so-called Peony path is a flower border, five or six feet wide. First a delicate line of Tulips is showing on the outer edge near the grass. These are Picotees, of the cottage type, white with a margin of rose pink. Next a double row of pink Peonies makes a brilliant showing. Then Pinks are spreading their grayish foliage and pink flowers over the gravel path. Then a row of Madonna Lilies gives the border its interest, and last, bronze Chrysanthemums with an edging of French Marigolds of the same peculiar shade make a finale in autumn tones. Each variety is planted throughout the length of the borders, but there is no set regularity, there are no hard straight lines that would give this planting an unpardonable stiffness. While they vary in color and flower habit, the uniformity of each effect gives the borders a simplicity appropriate for such a path, which acts as an introductory passage to the garden.

The Peony path meets at right angles the main garden path which runs across the entire width of the property, about 150 feet. Here the borders are very wide, ranging from ten to fifteen feet. Wide borders have a way of expressing the garden's luxuriance. On one side of this long cross path are the big Iris beds, on the other side are the mixed herbaceous borders. Despite the lack of uniformity of these two borders, there exists an underlying balance which is almost indefinable. Perhaps the reason for this fine adjustment is the consciousness that the first and principal view of the borders is from the back porch.

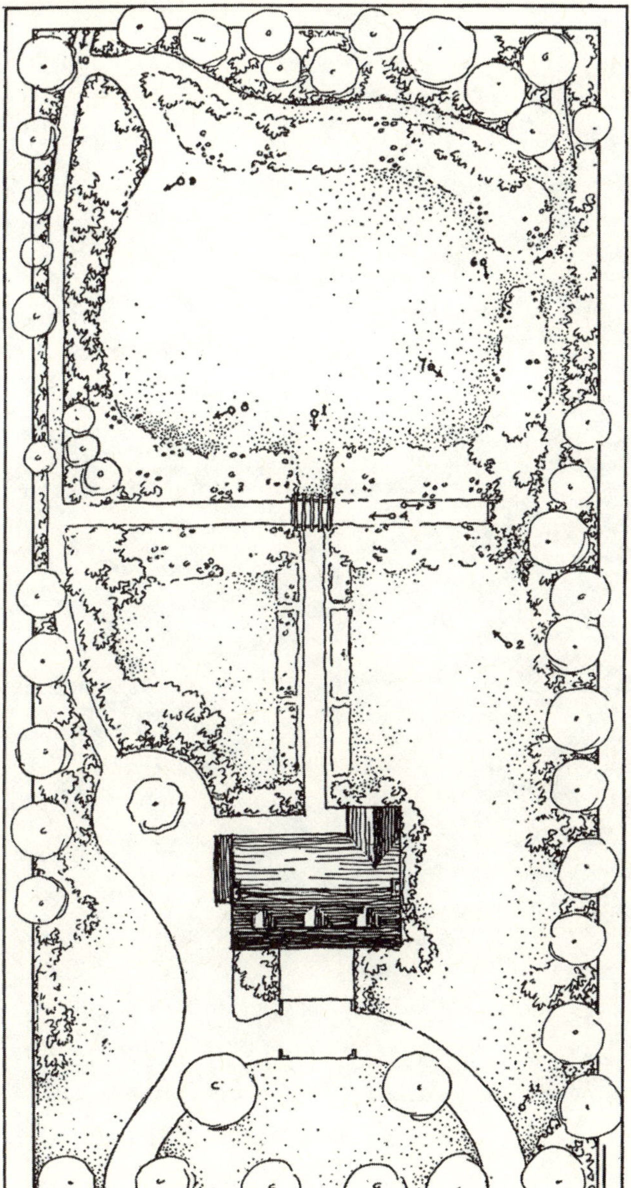

THE PLAN.

The Peony Walk.

The display of Irises lasts fully six weeks. First, there is a big show of Florentine Iris that makes a solid mass four feet wide. The Florentine Iris begin to bloom while the Darwin Tulips are still out. There are maroon Tulips, and black ones and cherry red ones, all mixed together to form an edge for the pearly Iris near the grass. On the path side Poet's Narcissus are planted for a very early spring effect. German Iris make the second big show in this border. There are the lilac blue *Iris pallida dalmatica*, the delicate creamy *Iris flavescens*, the golden *Iris aurea*, and Iris Dr. Bernice with yellow standards and deep bronze falls. These are planted in back of the Florentines, thirty or forty of each kind massed together. Just as the German Iris are fading, the Spanish Irises in yellow and smoky coloring are beginning to bloom, and at about the same time the English Irises in white and lilac blue shades. These make a delicate *intermezzo* before the third show of Japanese Irises. The Iris are massed so thickly that there is no room for other perennials except for a narrow row of edging plants.

At first Tree Peonies and standard Lilacs emphasized the intersection of the paths but now in addition to these a very simple rustic arbor has been built. It is heavily laden with climbing Roses, Gardenia, and Gold Finch, in yellow and coppery tones that repeat the color of the Hybrid Teas, Harry Kirk, and Madam Ravary, that are planted in three rows on either side of the arbor. Pansies that overrun these borders in the spring form a kind of irregular carpet bedding for the Roses. These Rose beds are incorporated in the big herbaceous borders, a daring attempt by any but a master hand.

These wide herbaceous borders are part and parcel of the enclosure of the main lawn which with their tree and shrubbery background comprise the garden proper. Here a charming color sequence is developed. The border at the back of the property, farthest from the house, is known as the red border, next to it is the purple and yellow border. A strong mass of Forsythia divides it from the blue border. The blue border ends where the Roses begin. On the other side of the Roses the pink border begins and that merges into white.

The method of producing this color sequence must not be misunderstood. There is no hard

Problem XI. No. 2.

The Main Garden Path.

Problem XI. No. 3.

The Iris Beds.

Problem XI. No. 3.

Standard Lilacs and Tree Peonies Marked the Intersection of the Paths before the Arbor was Built.

and fast color subdivision. In the so-called red border, there are not only red and scarlet flowers but those of orange and bronze shades. In the pink border, too, there are not only pink flowers but rose and maroon ones and even a few white ones. The red border is divided from the purple and yellow one by a strip of grass and so is the blue border divided from the pink one, but not into hard and distinct sections, for in looking over the whole garden area, one color seems to melt into the next color until they are blended and wrought into a rhythmic composition. It reminds one of a symphony in which each theme is introduced separately and then developed into complex harmonies. That is the trouble of trying to describe each border separately, we lose the effects of the other borders in so doing and we are apt to forget what an important part the trees and shrubs play. They act as a back drop to the scene, or to adhere to the comparison to the symphony, they are the strong accompaniment to the themes.

Take the red border. Its interest begins with early Tulips. With them are planted a few Crown Imperials, those curious favorites of old cottage gardens. At about the same time a few starry white Magnolias, *Magnolia stellata*, are in full bloom. Then come the later Tulips, the glowing red *Tulip gesneriana spathulata major*, the strong orange scarlet Tulip "La Merveille," and the showy Tulip "Pride of Haarlem." Then the red and yellow Azaleas bloom in a splendid mass in front of Hemlocks, then a group of Oriental Poppies make a brave showing and later in the fall red and bronze Dahlias and deep red Zinnias give a warm color touch that heralds the autumn glow of the Maples and Hawthorns in back of them.

The purple and yellow border is an exquisite study in flower arrangement and is especially charming in early May. Yellow *Alyssum saxatile* and Primroses and the lovely *Phlox lilacina* form the groundwork from which spring the Darwin and Cottage Tulips in similar shadings, the bright golden yellow Tulip "Mrs. Moon," the exquisite heliotrope Tulip "Dream," Tulip "Fairy Queen" in which heliotrope and yellow fawn color are blended, and the wonderful purple Tulip "Jubilee." The charm of this border does not depend wholly on the color harmony, wonderful as it is, not wholly upon the combination of ground cover and Tulips, but upon the composition of the whole. The edging plants grow in luxuriant intermingled mats

The Main Lawn.

The Purple and Yellow Border.

and the Tulips in big masses, a hundred or more of each kind planted in long irregular drifts magically blended. The composition is perhaps at its very best at the time when the tall long stemmed yellow Doronicums are also out and the lilac blue Camassias are beginning to bloom, for the Doronicums are scattered lightly between the Tulips, and a group of Camassias at the back provides a distinct accent point. It is interesting to note that in the fall the mood of the border has changed, for then dwarf and tall Heleniums make it a bright and bold corner.

When the Forsythias, that separate this border from the blue border, are blooming their yellow flowers bend down to meet deep yellow Daffodils and fine white *Arabis alpina* which are growing near by on the edge of the border. When flowering shrubs complement the flower color, combinations of rare interest arise and more charming opportunities in the use of shrubbery will open up when once we appreciate more fully their value and interest.

Soon after the Forsythia has leafed out, delicate tinted tulips are scattered through the blue border and in one corner there is a lovely blue mass of *Polemonium reptans*. Later *Linum perenne*, blue

Lupines, Anchusas, and Delphiniums carry along the blue effect while Gypsophila, *Anthemis kelwayi*, *Lilium svorzianum*, and yellow Thalictrums give touches of white, cream, yellow, and orange. Here, the plants are arranged in large irregularly interplanted clumps so that they blend the flower masses together. Such treatment seems to hide the plants out of bloom as they form drifts of foliage to offset the plants in bloom. By such methods the border seems always in full bloom for there are enough plants of each variety to give distinct effects.

In the pink border pink Lupines, pink Oriental Poppies, pink Sweet William, Canterbury Bells, and Hollyhocks follow one another in the spring and early summer, later on there are pink Phloxes and then Japanese Anemones give a delicate fall effect, but perhaps the finest time to see the pink border is at Tulip time. Then pink and white *Phlox subulata* is making a bright edging along the lawn and in back of it are the Tulips. There are the brilliant rose Tulip "Clara Butt," the soft rose Tulip "Loveliness," the exquisite dove-colored Tulip "The Fawn," and a few of the curious *Tulip viridiflora*, called the "Green Tulip." These are planted in broad masses

The Purple and Yellow Border when Tulips, Doronicums, Camassias, and Ground Covers are All in Bloom.

The Pink Border when the Crabapples and the Tulips are in Bloom.

where the border is wide and then they dwindle into a thin ribbon where the border becomes narrow. It seems, though, that this double effect of Tulips and ground Phlox is not enough, so a third element is added. The Tulips "Clara Butt" are planted in front of the Crabapple, *Pyrus floribunda*, whose pendant branches droop to the ground heavily laden with rose flowers. It is one of the loveliest tree and flower harmonies. There are many opportunities for such arrangements, especially in the spring with all the abundance of Almonds and Cherries, Crabapples and Dogwoods, Amelanchiers and Hawthorns. This is a field of artistic opportunity which we are just beginning to grasp. Farther down the border when the white flowering shrubs begin, there is another charming combination when creamy yellow *Iris pumila* is massed in front of a bush of *Spiræa thunbergii* bent with delicate white sprays.

This white flowering shrubbery helps to make the wood path which has its own little joys in shade-loving flowers. It is particularly lovely when the Foxgloves are out.

As the house is closed during midsummer and early fall, the garden contents itself with a few late autumn effects and a slight winter interest, so that all the attention can be centered upon the spring and early summer bloom. In the main garden the late Tulips make the first big showing, and a marvelous one it is with the complementary flowers of trees and shrubs and perennials, but the early spring is not forgotten. It is well taken care of in a place all its own, in the woodsy bulb border on the side of the house. There, Snowdrops and Winter Aconite, *Iris histrioides*, Chionodoxa, Grape-Hyacinth, Scillas, and the lovely lavender *Anemone blanda* are used in goodly masses, each group running into and mingling with the next. The first real height of bloom comes, however, with the crocuses when hundreds upon hundreds of them are planted not in solid stiff masses but in broad drifts that meander in graceful long easy curves through the border. A little later come the single star Daffodils planted in bolder streamerlike drifts. Later still, about the middle of May, the *Mertensia virginica*, the Virginia Cowslip, makes up the border's interest. This charming native has spires of nodding bell-like flowers that are delicate lilac blue that fades to soft pink.

Can we analyze this garden's charm? The

The White Border.

The Shady Path.

simplicity of the well ordered design, the nice sweeping curves of the lawns, the carefully studied background, the wide borders and the use of flowers in luxuriant naturalistic masses, all help toward its effectiveness. But necessary as these elements are, they are only the foundations. What is the elusive quality that makes a flower garden, like a symphony, a masterpiece? Can we define or describe the underlying meaning? A garden, if it is to be considered as a product of artistic value, must be a manifestation of distinctive individuality, an expression of personality.

PROBLEM XII

THE TERRACED GARDEN OF A COUNTRY PLACE, BY ELIZABETH BOOTES CLARK, LANDSCAPE ARCHITECT, PHILADELPHIA, PA.

This property is located at Devon, Pa. The dimensions of the garden are 36 x 80 feet

"BROOKMEAD" is an old country place. Its chief interest is centered upon the dairy farm. The whitewashed farm buildings stand close to the house, just on the other side of the drive, and the fine Guernsey cows find pasture on the broad sloping meadows that quite naturally usurp the greater part of the grounds and give the place its lovely rural character.

The house is low and old-fashioned. It is built of the gray stone that has given the country around Philadelphia its peculiar charm. The old driveway runs along the west of the house between groups of tall trees. A sloping piece of ground in front of the house is reserved as a kept lawn which is separated from the meadows by a white fence. On the other side of the house, the ground sloped off abruptly in an irregular double tilt that gave the house an unfortunate and unstable look. Part way down the slope a low retaining wall buttressed the ground. Such an awkward slope would not have appealed to the uninitiated as a good garden site but to one interested in the nice readjustments of grades such tilted contours are full of possibilities. It was on or rather into this bank that the garden was built in the fall of 1914.

The garden consists of two parts, a grass terrace and below it a series of small flower-lined compartments. The old retaining wall forms one boundary of the grass terrace. To conform with the grade it decreases gradually toward the south end and the terrace has a gentle downward slope in the same direction. To establish its grade it was necessary to cut away several feet of the slope. To conform with this new condition, the wall was underpinned, two feet at some places, eight feet at others. The old wall, built many years ago of rough stone with mortar of a brownish tone, is so fine a piece of work that matching up the stone, copying the laying of the courses, and imitating the

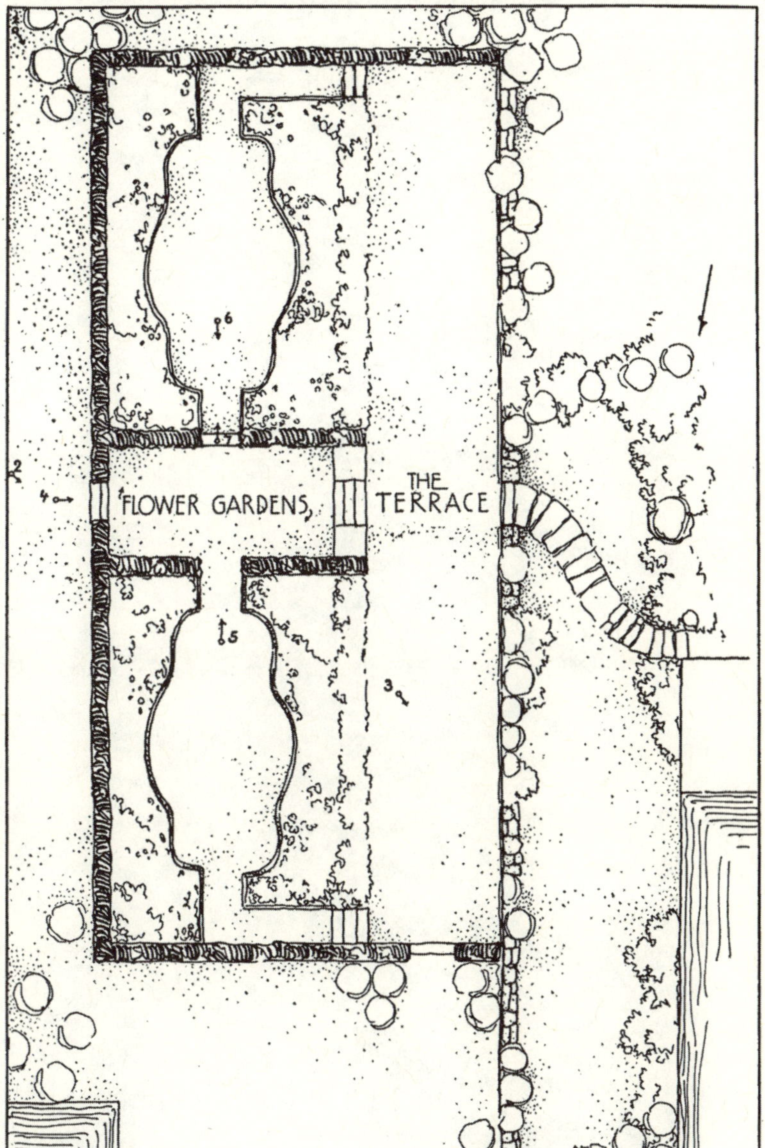

The Plan.

THE HOUSE AND THE GARDEN.

color of the mortar in building the new understructure demanded a certain nicety of feeling. The old quarry that furnished the stone for the house and for the old wall was unearthed on the place and it yielded the stone for all the new garden construction. The old spring house and outdoor oven, that stand beside the garden, are other examples of this fine old stone work that gives so much character to the place.

The retaining wall has given an interesting opportunity for wall planting. Sometimes it is pleasing to cover the entire wall with a hanging carpet of varied color, but here the plants are used only in a moderate way to soften the bareness of the stone without hiding the wall. The wall is so long, however,—about eighty feet,—that many different kinds of plants are used in small groups. The flowers are there, not to demand undivided attention, but are to solicit momentary interest. They are used, not as a dominant feature, but as a decorative touch of color.

Cedars, *Juniperus virginiana glauca*, border the other long side of the terrace. When they spread into a continuous boundary, the terrace will attain all the cool and shadow flickered charm of a bowling green.

In contrast to the quiet green of the terrace, the garden is a study in full color. It is set parallel to the terrace at a slightly lower level and consists of three subdivisions. The central portion acts as a thoroughfare. It is centered on the middle of the terrace. It is in line with the curving steps that run up to the porch. It is in line with the gate that opens into the pasture. It is simply a grass space enclosed by Arbor Vitæ hedges. A small blue green bowl stands in the grass for a bird bath. Two chairs stand by the side of the steps to the terrace. These chairs remind one of the colonial Windsors but they are English. They are designed especially for English weather for after a shower the chair can be turned upside down and be right side up to provide a clean dry seat.

On the sides of this green space are the two flower compartments. The upper garden is two steps above, the lower garden is two steps below it. In this way has the difference in grade, uniform with the terrace slope, been pleasingly dealt with. The upper garden is mottled with shadow, the lower garden is in full sunlight. The upper garden has a background of tall trees that group themselves around the spring house, the lower garden faces the sunny meadows and high up on a tall

Problem XII. No. 2.

The Entrance from the Meadow.

Problem XII. No. 3.

The Terrace.

Between the Two Color Gardens.

white pole a bird house stands outlined against the sky. In the upper garden the flowers are of pastel shades, in the lower garden the flowers are brighter in key, blues that deepen into purple and the yellows that tone to orange with a touch of pure white. In the early spring the borders of both gardens are fringed with Crocuses in mixed colors and Daffodils and early Tulips. It is not, however, until the later long-stemmed Tulips appear that the gardens show their full color values. Then in the upper garden, many varieties are woven into a delicate color rhythm. There are pure white Tulips, "White Queen," and pink striped "Picotee," silvery rose "Gretchen" and lilac rose "Mme. Krelage." There are bright pink Tulips, "Clara Butt," and salmon ones, "Inglescombe Pink." There are golden Tulips, "Bouton d'Or," heliotrope, "Dream," and "The Fawn" which is dove colored. In the lower garden the bright shades of *Tulip gesneriana lutea* and of "Inglescombe Yellow" offset the quieter tones of "Dream," of the slaty blue "La Tristesse," of the dark plum colored "Philippe de Commines," and of the red purple "Mrs. Potter Palmer." While the Tulips are blooming the Columbines, scattered through both gardens in mixed colors, are beginning to flower. A little later salmon pink Oriental Poppies, "Mrs. Perry," are flowering in the upper garden and their bloom is followed by Canterbury Bells. At almost the same time Spanish Iris are blooming in the lower garden. On one side they are blue and white, on the other side they are white and yellow.

When considered as a mass, the flowers have, so far, given a flat effect, but as summer approaches perpendicular lines begin to predominate. In the upper garden there are masses of pink Foxgloves and lovely blue Anchusas with smaller groups of the delicate pink *Lilium krameri.* In the lower garden the Larkspurs emphasize the perpendicular lines. In bloom with them are the white Madonna Lilies, the orange Lilies, *Lilium croceum*, and yellow Thermopsis. The familiar combination of *Lilium candidum* with Delphinium is strong and pure, the union of Larkspurs and orange Lilies gives a warm and rich color harmony.

Then there is a slight lull until the Phloxes begin to bloom. Lilac rose Phlox "Mme. Dutrie" and soft violet Phlox "Wanadis" make a delicate union for the pastel garden. Only pure white Phlox "Mrs. Jenkins" and "Jeanne D'Arc" are used in the other garden. Aconitum and orange *Lilium superbum* carry out the color harmony of the lower

Problem XII. No. 5.

The Blue and Yellow Garden.

Problem XII. No. 6.

The Pastel Garden.

Another View of the Blue and Yellow Garden.

garden for a time, but when the blue is lost in late autumn, yellow and bronze Chrysanthemums are left to carry along the bright part of the color scheme. The upper garden adheres to pastel shades during the early fall with pink and white Japanese Anemones, pink and cream *Gladiolus gandavensis*, and steel blue Sea Holly.

It is essential to describe the gardens together, for, despite the fact that each garden makes a distinct color impression, the two color schemes are in harmony for the two gardens are complimentary parts of one closely knit design. Their unity is further emphasized by their strong structural similarity. They are alike in shape and size. Each has a tiny grass center edged in quaint oval outlines with dwarf Box. Each has its own entrance from the terrace above. Each has a little nook with a seat in it. These seats are long low benches. They were found in an antique shop. They are made of Irish bog oak that was petrified through the action of water. They have no need of paint so their natural soft brownish tone can always be preserved.

The terrace and the garden seem perfectly at home tucked in there under the wall. They are sunk so far below the house that even when the hedges grow to full height the view from the house across the meadows will be free and the garden detail will not disturb the open feeling of the meadows. They are easily reached from the dining room and porch by two flights of steps, and so are closely united to the house. Full of sunlight and color, full of shadow and restful green, the garden and terrace are quiet out-of-door rooms, a charming addition to the house interpreting in their own peculiar manner the prevailing character of the house. Such an achievement in garden art is due to an intuitive feeling of fitness, to a sense of "perfect placing" which gives to that which is the object of infinite care and anxious thought the appearance of perfect naturalness.

PROBLEM XIII

A SMALL PROPERTY WITH TWO GARDENS, BY ELIZABETH LEONARD STRANG, LANDSCAPE ARCHITECT, GROTON, MASS.

This property is located at Plymouth, Mass. Its dimensions are 165 x 150 feet

IN the development of the small lot the attention is best centered upon one important feature. This feature should be in full sight of the house and have a close relationship to it. It should have individuality and worth enough to perpetuate genuine pleasure in it. It should have elasticity enough to offer a chance for the expression of changing and growing interests. It should have a distinct originality which will grow in the hands of an ingenious designer directly out of some character peculiar to the site itself.

These principles underlie the development of this property. The unobtrusive low shrubbery, still rather unconvincing in its newness, which is planted along the front of the house, together with the quiet character of the house itself, conforms with the simple Plymouth street overshadowed by old Elms. The front of the house has nothing of particular interest. The attention is focused upon the garden in back.

In the beginning it was only a deep uninviting hollow. Now it is an oval flower garden. In May, 1913, it was an unsightly dump, an ugly hole in the ground. In August of the same year there was a carefully arranged garden with abundant bloom and color which convinces one of the efficiency of a plan by which the work is carried on skillfully and rapidly without the unnecessary readjustments of haphazard and disjointed ideas.

Its oval shape and symmetrical treatment fit naturally into its sunken position. Its full expanse is seen in a semi-bird's-eye view from the house. The path on the shorter axis of the oval, centering on the central doorway and terminating in the generous seat under the trees, binds house and garden together. A path on the longer axis meets it in a circle at the center, cutting the oval into four equal parts. The main lines of the design have a simplicity of which one cannot tire. They have a strength which holds together all the

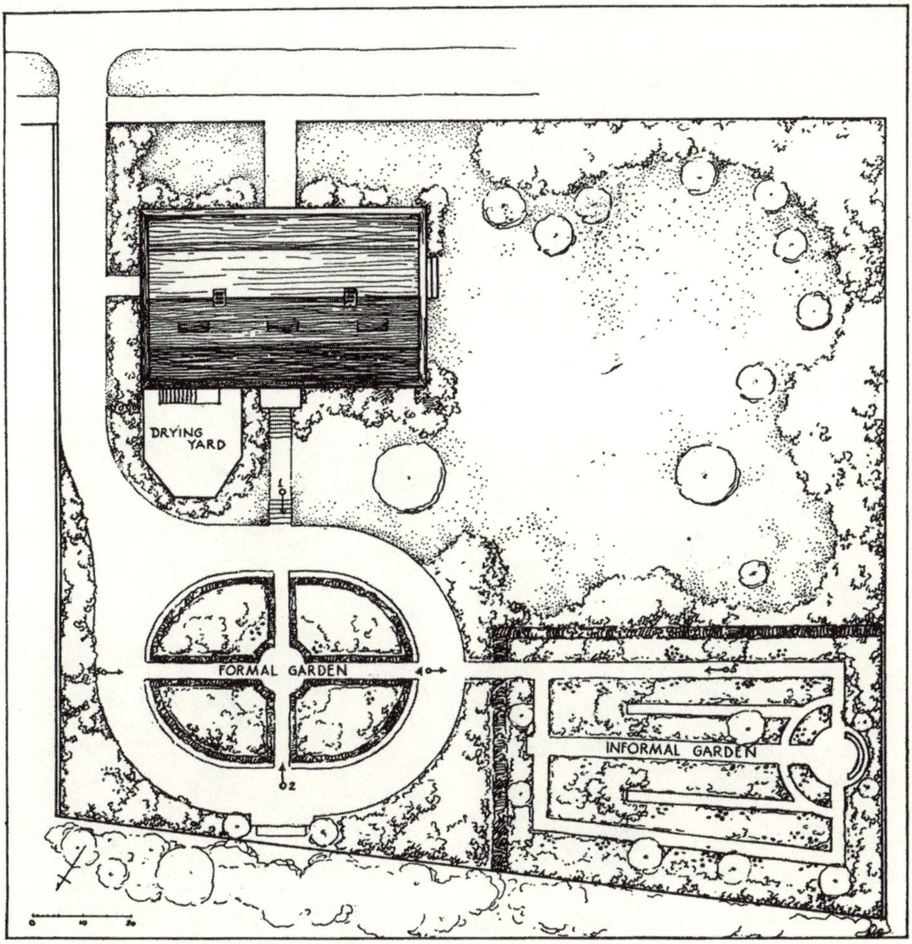

The Plan.

The House and the Formal Garden.

minor elements. For convenience in caring for the flowers in the very wide borders a stepping stone path describes an inner oval. In summer it is almost lost in the thickness of the foliage but in spring it strikes a minor chord in the composition.

The flowers are arranged to carry out and emphasize the design. The four parts of the oval are so planted that at first glance they appear symmetrically correct. In early spring this effect is gained by the careful distribution of early flowers. Daffodils skirt the outer edge of the oval, Scillas and Snowdrops, Primulas and Fritillarias are planted between the stepping stones, early pink and rose Tulips and Mertensias circumscribe the circle, and lavender Darwin Tulips describe a wider circle around them. A little later in the season the effect of symmetry is continued by dividing equally between the four parts masses of Irises and Peonies, Phloxes and Japanese Anemones, Asters and Chrysanthemums. Planted in strong masses they give body to the borders. The monotony of absolute conformity is avoided, however, by subtle gradations of color made possible through the abundant use of many named varieties. Moreover, no exact symmetry is attempted in the placing of the many other flowers that are used in small quantities to lighten the strong mass effect.

A balanced arrangement of flowers is quite rigidly adhered to in the borders on either side of the short path. Throughout its length, English Daisies and early Tulips make a continuous border in early spring to be followed by Forget-me-Nots. In back of them is a row of salmon pink Sweet William whose June flowers are replaced by the later bloom of Heliotrope and pink Stock. The white and pink Peonies in back of the Sweet William in the nearer borders are substituted by the yellowish blush Pæony canari farther away. A balanced effect is also felt in the arrangement of the flowers on either side of the longer path. Bordered by *Alyssum saxatile* and Arabis, Adonis and white Wild Geranium, Carpathian Harebell, Statice, and Sedum, the edge is kept in almost continuous bloom. The varying greens and gray greens of the foliage add a special interest to these compact matlike ground covers. In back of this edging of dwarf flowers, Iris "Queen of May," *Iris pallida,* and Iris "Purple King" range from soft lilac pink through lilac to deep purple. At the circle the symmetry is most strictly

The Formal Garden.

PROBLEM XIII. No. 3.

THE LONGER AXIS OF THE FORMAL GARDEN.

carried out. This is done to focus the attention upon the central point and so bind together the many motives of the flower design. The planting is arranged in a series of inscribed circles. In the first ring early Mertensias make a complete circle with blue flowers that fade to pink. These are replaced later on by deep purple Pansies. During July this tier is made effective by eight *Œnothera missouriensis* placed at the points where the paths converge into the circle. Their large bright yellow flowers make a brilliant showing, especially striking in front of the deep purple of Japanese Iris. In the second ring Iris "Purple King" continues the color effect of the purple Pansies. In the third ring are Peonies in deep pink and rose. Each Peony is encircled by a dozen pink Tulips whose early flowers have disappeared by the time the Peony has opened its foliage. In the fourth ring are the purple Japanese Iris. With them the circular treatment fades into the masses of Phlox which help to develop the oval outlines of the garden.

It is obvious that in such a garden the continuity of bloom is most carefully developed. Early Tulips, Daffodils, Darwin Tulips and Irises, Peonies and Sweet Williams, Foxgloves, Larkspurs and Phloxes,

Japanese Anemones and Asters, and Chrysanthemums give successive bloom. Coming into flower one after another with varying lengths to their periods of bloom they are closely interwoven and used in big masses they form the major succession of bloom. Complementing them is a minor succession. Bright yellow Alyssum, pure white Arabis, blue Mertensia, pink Bleeding Heart, yellow Trollius make a spring medley of bright color. Columbines and yellow Day Lilies accompany the bloom of German Irises, Dictamnus and Campanulas that of the Peonies. Purple *Viola cornuta*, snow-white Achillea "the Pearl," and filmy Gypsophila accompany the flowering of the Larkspurs. Yellow Anthemis, pink *Sedum spectabile*, blue Statice, and purple Veronicas are in flower while the Phloxes are blooming. Pink Snapdragons supplement the delicacy of Japanese Anemones, salmon pink annual Phlox continues to bloom late into Aster time, and Calendulas are still fresh when the last Chrysanthemum has faded. Supplementing the major succession, these scattered color notes, sometimes strong, sometimes very delicate, heighten the interest in the changes that come from week to week. Special attention has been given to color in this garden. Not a single harsh or disturbing color note can be found. Only the clearest of yellows, the softest of pink and rose shades, the quietest of lavender, blue, and purple, and harmonizing whites are used in this elusive pattern of color. Succession of bloom, color harmony, and arrangement are subtly interwoven. Thus analyzed the garden illustrates the difficulties and the pleasures of its designing. It makes clear the reason for many failures, the source of its many delights.

It is as easy to enumerate the flowers planted in a garden as it is hard to describe the elusive effects that are attained. It is as simple to explain the underlying principles of the garden's composition as it is difficult to analyze its charm. A flower garden is a transitory evanescent thing. Without constant, patient, and intelligent care the whole charm of a garden like this one, dependent on so many interrelated details, is lost in a year's time. This garden has the frequent supervision of the designer. This means not only that she can see that it is kept up to the color scheme and arrangement as she divined it, that she can foretell and forewarn lapses in bloom, winter failures, and seasonal mishaps, but she can arrange and complete, substitute and devise new color effects in minor details which will give new interest to the garden without disturbing its old vigor and its stable and constant arrangement.

The oval is Box bordered and then girt by a ten-foot strip of gravel. Although we had carefully studied the plan of the entire layout beforehand, we had been altogether unconscious throughout the long and minute inspection of the oval, that the gravel strip was a turn-around. A turn-around is so much a matter for practical considerations, a flower garden is so much a striving for an ideal, and the two seem so antagonistic that they are almost always placed entirely apart from one another. It is at best, even for so small a place where the drive turn is in little use, a difficult problem and a combination which is to be avoided. In this case, however, the harmonizing of these two opposing factors strikes not only a clever and original note in garden composition but shows a serious understanding of garden art.

Besides developing the principal feature of a place there is often a possibility of combining with it a number of other scenes of special character. By the addition of the neighboring property,

At the Entrance of the Informal Garden.

Problem XIII. No. 5.

In the Informal Garden.

space for a lawn and an informal garden was acquired. The property was bought in two parcels—the lawn area came into possession only recently, the informal garden was planted at the time the formal garden was laid out.

The lawn is bordered by a woodsy plantation. The Rhododendrons and Hemlocks, opposite the porch, are flanked by groups of Black Alder and *Viburnum dentatum*, Fragrant Sumac and Maple-leaved Viburnum, *Cornus paniculata*, Cornelian Cherry and Red Twigged Cornel, Barberries *Rosa multiflora* and Mountain Ash, *Viburnum Carlesi*, Laurel, and *Ilex glabra*, which is a charming and little known variety of Holly. They unite to form a planting with fine autumn and winter effects. Spring wood flowers, Ferns and Asters, *Azalea vaseyi* and Oriental Poppies, *Lilium Hansoni* and Snakeroot, form interesting color incidents for the heavier shrub planting.

The informal garden occupies a narrow irregular strip of sloping land in back of the lawn. One of the long paths of this garden is a continuation of the longer axis of the main garden. The rose arch which acts as entrance to it frames a long vista down the path. This minor garden is subordinated to the main garden but it is related to it. It is as informal as the other is formal. It is left to the lax attention of odd moments instead of to the diligent care and constant supervision given to the main garden. It is as unsymmetrical in design and planting as the other is symmetrical.

Japanese Quinces and Bush Roses, old-fashioned Sweet-scented Shrub and Bush Honeysuckles, fragrant Mock Oranges and Weigelas are scattered through the ample beds to obstruct the view across the garden.

Many flowers grow rampant in the borders and encroach upon the paths with their spreading foliage. There are Hepaticas, Wind Flowers, Bloodroots, and other spring wild flowers. There are Snowdrops and Lilies-of-the-Valley, double Buttercups and Snow-in-Summer with lovely gray foliage. There are spring bulbs, Narcissus and Tulips, Spanish Iris and *Fritillaria meleagris* (the speckled Guinea-hen Flower). There are summer bulbs, Madonna Lilies, Gold-banded Lilies, nodding Japanese Lilies, and brilliant Tiger Lilies. There are many-colored Gladioli.

A few Oriental Poppies blaze forth their scarlet all alone amid dark green foliage; Lychnis and Monarda, Heuchera (the Coral Bell) and Lobelia (the Cardinal Flower), each has a special place where its color will not hurt more delicate shades or be hurt by them.

There are delicate filmy flowers like Gypsophila, Galium, and Statice and tropical-looking plants like Yuccas. There are all kinds of Campanulas, Harebells, Bell Flowers, and Peach Bells. There are all kinds of spiked flowers, pyramidal Foxgloves, spires of Larkspurs and Monkshoods, Hollyhocks, and coarse-leaved Physostegia with spikes of gaping flowers, some purple, some lilac, some white. There are sturdy Anchusas with azure flowers, decorative Shasta Daisies, flat-headed Anthemis, and luxurious Phloxes. There are feathery plumes of Thalictrums and odd Sea Holly with blue thistle-like globes on blue stems with spiny blue-green foliage.

There are summer wild flowers, Orange Milkweed from the sandy roadsides, white Eupatoriums from the fields, strong yellow Mulleins from stony hillsides, and delicate Evening Primroses. Large white *Boltonia asteroides*, tall reddish purple New England Asters, and sturdy Yellow Heleniums make strong autumn color.

There are all kinds of annuals, Ageratum and Scabiosa, white Petunias and blue Nigellas, Heliotrope and Cosmos, purple Pansies and brilliant orange Zinnias, pink annual Larkspurs and salmon pink Phlox, lemon yellow and orange Marigolds and Mignonettes, Snapdragons and lovely scented Stocks. Pots of tender flowers, sweet smelling Lemon Verbena and Rose Geranium, are plunged in the ground.

It is a place for old-fashioned plants and favorites, flowers of odd colors and curious shapes. It is a medley of color, a spot full of fragrance. Little surprises are at every turn, unexpected flowers are found in hidden corners. There are blind paths where steps have to be retraced through little flower tangles. It has absorbed in a very short time the indescribable old-fashioned quality of a colonial garden.

PROBLEM XIV

An Old Place on Level Ground—Redesigned, by Charles N. Lowrie, Landscape Architect, New York City

This property is located at Columbus, Ohio. Its dimensions are 250 x 400 feet

IT becomes more and more necessary, as houses crowd closer together in a city, to consider each property as a unit in itself, and to disregard all heterogeneous outside objects. To do this satisfactorily it is important to hide the close proximity of neighboring houses. The making of the boundary is, therefore, very essential. Here, the boundary is doubly fortified. A brick wall is built around three sides of the property with a hedge on the front, for a green hedge forms a much pleasanter boundary along the street than a wall. Inside wall and hedge is a planting of trees and shrubbery which disguises their stiff lines, gives height to the enclosure, and affords pleasant variation in color and form.

The location of the old house and of existing trees determined the development of the front part of the grounds. The attractive lawn on the east side of the house gains its interest through the careful grouping of trees and the good shape of the curving plantations that form the boundary. On the west side of the house there is just room enough for a drive. It enters from the street on the very edge of the property and curves slightly on the way to the porte-cochère. This is an excellent arrangement, for a drive on a small property ought to be merely a convenience and take up as little room as possible. It plays, however, an important part of the layout as a friendly entrance to the house and is to be as attractive as good lines and planting can make it.

The old brown stone houses of the seventies do not lend themselves happily to garden settings, nor was there then any understanding of the garden as an intimate part of the house so there was no attempt to establish the new garden near the house. Happily the tall growth of existing trees that help to make the garden setting hide the house from the garden. The only connection

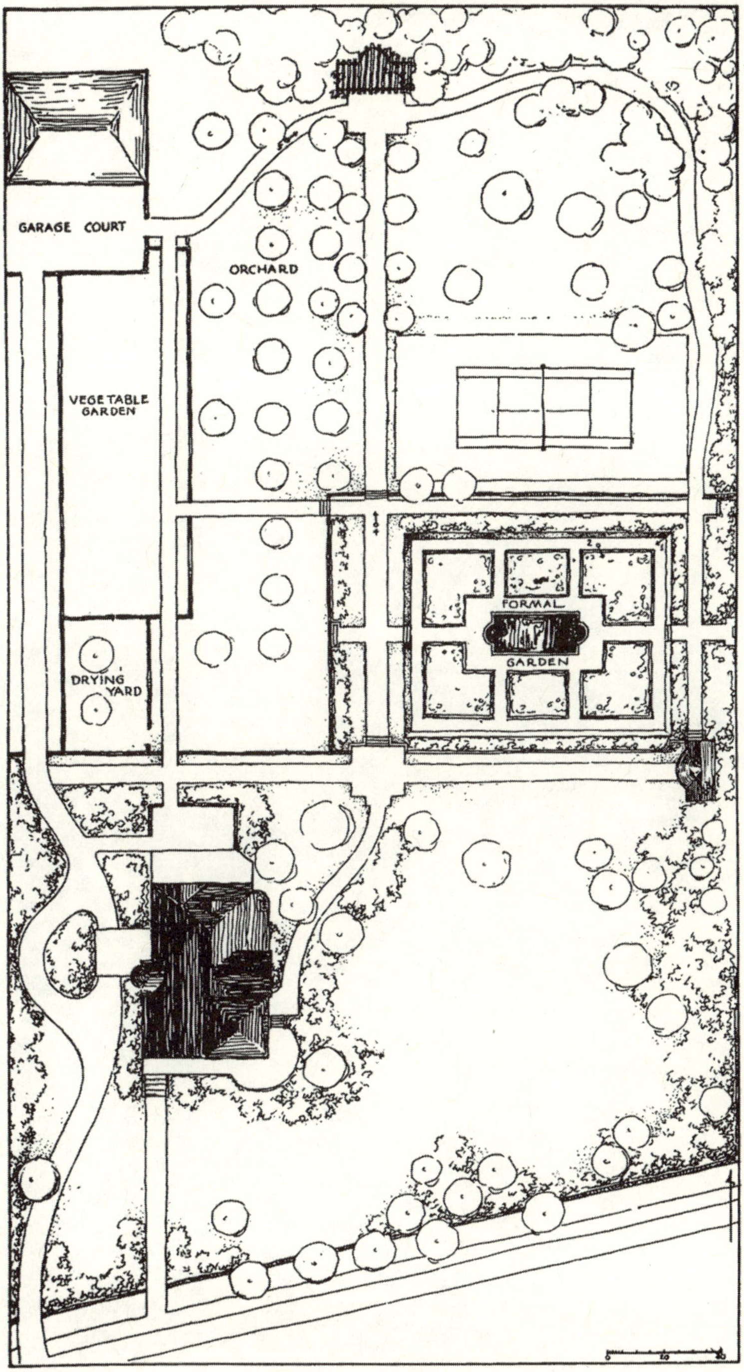
GARAGE COURT
ORCHARD
VEGETABLE GARDEN
FORMAL
GARDEN
DRYING YARD

The Plan.

The Garden.

between house and garden is a curving path. This path connects with two other paths which are at right angles to one another, a short east and west path which has a tea house at its eastern end and a long north and south path at the end of which the pergola is seen through an avenue of flowering Crabapples. This long path forms an axis line through the center of the property. The separation of the house and its garden and the seeming disregard of attempting to establish a unity between the house and the layout of the grounds is explained by the fact that, at the time the grounds were developed, it was the expectation of the owner to remove the existing house and to place a new one so that its axis line would conform to that of the centrally located path.

This long path divides the property into two equal parts. On the west side is the service portion, the road to the garage, the hedge-bounded vegetable garden, laundry yard, and the orchard. On the east side is the social part, the formal garden with its rose center, the tennis court, the play lawn with its fruit trees, the tea house, and the shady informal path which connects tea house and pergola and then with a curve which disguises entirely its intention turns into the court in front of the garage. It is an essential of good planning that the service part be cut off and entirely hidden from the garden and yet there should be easy access between them. In fact it is essential to have easy communication between all the various parts of the grounds and there is an added interest if in the leisurely inspection of the grounds there need be no retracing of steps.

In choosing the site for the garden it is interesting to note that the existing orchard and old trees were not disturbed. In order to relieve the flatness of the property of its monotony, several slight changes in level were made in the garden design. The Box bordered Rose beds in the center help to emphasize the sunken garden effect and the perennial borders around them form a transition between the low Roses and the tall trees behind. All the main paths are of gravel but these in the formal garden are of grass. Such changes in material help to make attractive gardens. The seats, vases, and statues in the garden are the owner's own collection and although it is difficult to arrange for so many different objects so that they will fit together the simple broad formal design of the garden, the simplicity of the pool, and the

Problem XIV. No. 2.

The Tea House.

Problem XIV. No. 3.

Inside the Tea House.

Problem XIV. No. 4.

The Long Path.

Problem XIV. No. 5.

The Pergola.

frame of trees make a quiet setting for them. The tea house, too, is built in a dignified classic style for this reason.

It is interesting to note that all the ornamentation has been reserved for this formal garden as it is the center of attraction. The rest of the grounds are kept quite simple. The fruit trees were part of an old orchard and show how nicely such existing material can be woven into the design. The pergola is the center of interest in the orchard and it forms a quiet informal lounging place. It is built in a simple modern style quite different from the tea house. Side by side in the same garden they would be incongruous but placed as they are in no connection with one another they both fill their places well.

In the shrubbery and trees that bound the various subdivisions there are many interesting details of planting: there is a continuous succession of bloom, much contrast of foliage texture and bright winter color. It is this color of fruit and branches in deciduous plant material which provides so much of the winter effectiveness of a garden quite independent of the evergreens that so often dominate and overbalance it but here the evergreens have been used sparingly except in the boundary plantings where White Pines and Hemlocks make a permanent screen and are an effective background to the color of shrub and flower.

PROBLEM XV

A HILLSIDE PROPERTY IN A NEW ENGLAND TOWN, BY PRENTICE SANGER, LANDSCAPE ARCHITECT, NEW YORK CITY

This property is located at Fitchburg, Mass. Its dimensions are 300 x 600 feet

THE sharp and peculiar double tilt of the property to the south and to the west, the distant view of the hills to the southwest, and the position of house and barn were the conditions which determined the solution of this problem. The demand for a garden on the south side necessitated an arrangement of terraces to suit the steep slope and the northern position of the kitchen wing and of the new garage placed on the barn foundations determined the rearrangement of the drive.

A "home-ground" is an organism in which the subdivisions, while serving their own peculiar functions, are united into one harmonious whole.

It is, therefore, not merely a problem of ornamental planting, as it is often supposed, but a solution of practical conditions molded into a skillful design and supplemented by a planting of decorative value.

The front lawn is kept quite simple and in harmony with the character of a New England town. The old trees just inside the wall which extends along the street give abundant shade and a finished appearance to the planting. The stiff line of the wall is broken by masses of Laurel under the trees. Two old Maples fortunately placed on either side of the entrance path make an unusually fine setting for the gateway. The tree and shrubbery planting which frames in the south side of the lawn disguises somewhat the steep slope and has an added value in helping to enclose the flower garden, screening it from the street.

The drive is a frank piece of necessary construction. It takes the place of an old drive which had described a semicircle in front of the house with two entrances on the street. This had made a considerable mass of gravel not pleasant to look

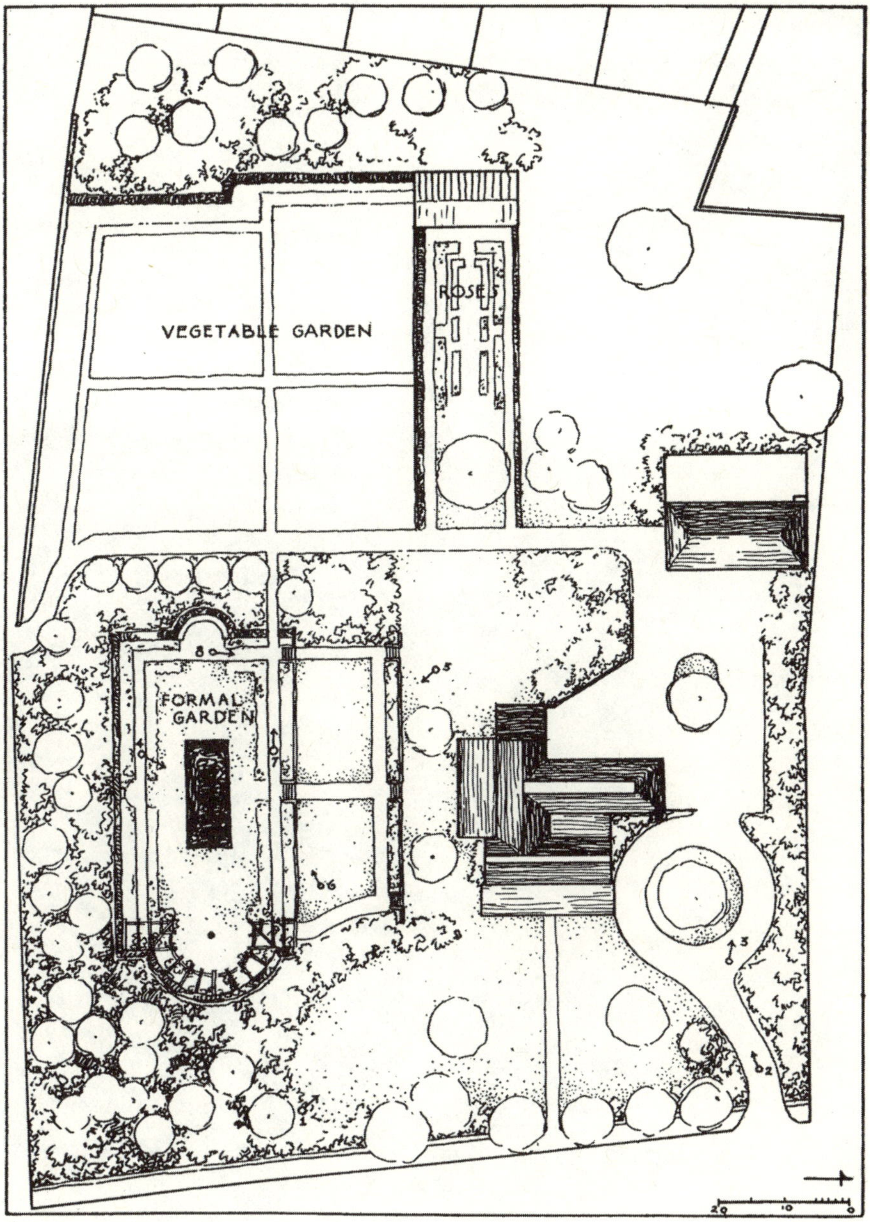

The Plan.

The House.

at and brought the drive very near the garden side of the house. Both these objectionable conditions were obviated by the new drive. It is on the extreme northern side of the lot so that it does not encroach on any other part of the grounds. It takes up the least possible space but gives generous room for turning. It is in close and direct communication with service court and garage. Near the entrance of the drive on the lawn side Prairie Roses and prostrate Junipers spread their branches over outcropping rocks. On the other side the pendant branches of Forsythia and the graceful growth of Spiræa bring the taller shrubbery down to the ground. At the back a trellis divides the drive from the service court.

It is always well to screen the service court from the rest of the grounds but it is a pity to hide too much a building so charming in exterior as the garage. It is not often that we find so much architectural consideration given to a subordinate building on a property. The garage has two entrances and ample room for two cars besides the usual outfit rooms. The barn's stone foundation upon which it is built forms good storage room below and provides a large additional space in back, on the garage level, for an open balustraded platform useful for cleaning the machines. The small grove of old White Pines is especially picturesque in relation to the garage which it shades. The service court is also used as a laundry yard. This combination is excellent economy of space for small properties.

From the service court a narrow service road runs between vegetable plot and formal garden to a side entrance. The main street is so very steep that it is desirable to have even a slightly less steep service road. The rose garden is treated more as a cut-flower garden than as a garden for ornamental purposes. In this capacity it subordinates itself to the main garden and ranks more with the vegetable garden. The vegetable plot is at so much lower level that although it is in easy communication with the rest of the grounds it stands quite apart. The service road and the steep grade so effectively divide the vegetable and rose gardens from the grounds immediately around the house that while they are molded into the general scheme it would be quite possible to omit them entirely without losing any sense of the general unity which the arrangement of lawn, drive, service court, and garden gives to the grounds. The extreme western portion of the property—

Problem XV. No. 2.

The Turn-Around.

Problem XV. No. 3.

The Service Court and Garage.

Problem XV. No. 4.

The House and the Garden.

only partly indicated on the plan—is again at so much lower level than the vegetable garden that it has no connection at all with the "home-ground." Houses could be built on it without disturbing the view of the hills. For this reason the landscape architect advised selling this portion. The subdivision into lots would give five fifty-foot lots of good depth. The plot is, however, not on the market but presents at this time a forest of baby White Pines.

The steep slope on the south side of the house became the site for the garden. Such abrupt changes in level put strict limitations on a property but they are welcome factors in garden making. In making use of such a property a series of artificial levels becomes necessary. Terraces offer great variety in treatment, but in their making the cost of digging out and filling in of soil is a practical element that is weighed in the balance with the artistic elements of the design.

Here, the highest level is the lawn in front of the living room, the second level is a green parterre, and the lowest level is the formal flower garden. Along one side of the lawn is a planting of *Abies concolor*, *Juniperus prostrata*, and *Rosa nitida*.

These are particularly interesting in autumn and winter when the red of the Rose stems makes a contrasting note with the gray green of the Spruce. *Juniperus tameriscifolia*, one of the numerous forms of the prostrate Juniper, plays a delightful little part at intervals against the brick steps of the piazza.

Between the lawn and the parterre is a wall surmounted with a balustrade. Below the wall is a flower border. The parterre is the intermediate space between the house terrace and the sunny flower garden. Three stairs with accompanying paths lead down through it to the garden.

The boundary of *Abies concolor* and *Rosa nitida* on the lawn is continued with Ghent Azaleas against Arbor Vitæ on the parterre and with *Pyrus atrosanguinea* against White Spruce in the garden. The Hawthorn hedge which encloses three sides of the garden is another interesting feature. In back of the Hawthorn hedge evergreen and deciduous trees are massed into a heavy plantation and disguise somewhat the irregular slope of the ground as it drops away from the garden level. They form a generous boundary for the garden. The varying green of White Spruce, Cedars, Scotch Pine, White Pine, and Hemlocks makes a pleasant

Problem XV. No. 5.

The Terrace and the Garden.

Problem XV. No. 6.

The Pool.

Problem XV. No. 7.

The Semi-Circular Seat.

Problem XV. No. 8.

The Gateway.

contrast with the flowers, while the flowering trees, Amelanchier, Redbud, Dogwood, Locust, Yellow-Wood, Horse-Chestnut, and Catalpa, add to the bloom and color of perennials.

The privacy gained by a good enclosure is very essential in the success of the garden as an out-of-door room. The large semicircular seat on the west side of the garden is a very inviting place from which to view the flowers. When the Hemlocks at its back are tall enough to throw the shadow of delicate boughs across it, it will grow in charm and seclusion. Opposite to the seat is the pergola. It is fortunate in its position in front of the heavy evergreen planting. As soon as the vines begin to cover it, it will sink into its right place and be a shady retreat from which to look out on the sunny flower borders. There is a seat opposite the central stairway to the garden. It is quite delicate in effect, especially in contrast to the large seat. It is rather suggestive of an indoor settee while the large seat has the solidity more frequently found in stone construction than in wood. Careful arrangement of seats to provide vantage points for the leisurely inspection of the flowers is important in the design of this size.

The four central flower beds form the borders

for the lawn space and for the pool in its center. The oblong shape of the pool conforms with the rectangular outline of the garden. It is interesting to note that the pool is so constructed that the grass can grow to the very edge of the water. The effect is particularly good in preserving the simplicity of the lawn. The central beds are comparatively low and broad in appearance; the long side borders give an enclosing high effect.

A certain balance and unity in the flower distribution is essential for a formal garden but the mixed herbaceous borders give a welcome informality to the straight lines of the paths and beds. The riotous and continuous bloom of many varieties is very effective when the garden is viewed from above and adds an interest to the close inspection of the flowers when one comes unexpectedly upon scattered groups of them.

The garden is an intimate part of the house, especially of the living room. Its sheltered position, its comfortable seats, its shady nooks, its bright color draw one out of the room. The unity between house and garden is so close, despite the difference of level, that it is not appreciated that the garden was built first and the house then rebuilt with the garden in view. The stereotyped arrangement of rooms in the old house, necessary in days when all the "best" rooms had to face the street, was changed so that the large homey living room could face upon the garden.

INDEX